Past Masters
General Editor Keith Thomas

Kant

Roger Scruton is Professor of Philosophy and University Professor at Boston University. His books include *Spinoza*, also in the Past Masters series, *Sexual Desire*, and *Modern Philosophy*, along with several works of fiction.

Past Masters

Forthcoming

Roger Scruton

Kant

Oxford   New York

OXFORD UNIVERSITY PRESS

Oxford University Press, Walton Street, Oxford OX2 6DP

Oxford New York
Athens Auckland Bangkok Bombay
Calcutta Cape Town Dar es Salaam Delhi
Florence Hong Kong Istanbul Karachi
Kuala Lumpur Madras Madrid Melbourne
Mexico City Nairobi Paris Singapore
Taipei Tokyo Toronto

and associated companies in
Berlin Ibadan

Oxford is a trade mark of Oxford University Press

First published 1982 as an Oxford University Press paperback
Reissued 1996

British Library Cataloguing in Publication Data
Data available

Library of Congress Cataloging in Publication Data
Scruton, Roger.
Kant.—(Past masters)
1. Kant, Immanuel.
I. Title.   II. Series.
193 B2798
ISBN 0-19-287578-7
ISBN 0-19-287577-9 Pbk

20 19 18 17 16 15 14 13 12 11

Printed in Great Britain by
Biddles Ltd
Guildford and King's Lynn

Preface

I have tried to present Kant's thought in a modern idiom, while presupposing the least possible knowledge of philosophy. Since Kant is one of the most difficult of modern philosophers, I cannot hope that I have made every aspect of this thought intelligible to the general reader. It is not clear that every aspect of his thought has been intelligible to *anyone*, even to Kant. The depth and complexity of Kant's philosophy are such that it is only after complete immersion that the importance of its questions, and the imaginative power of its answers, can be understood. Kant hoped to draw the limits of the human understanding; he found himself compelled to transcend them. The reader should therefore not be surprised if he has to read this introduction more than once in order to appreciate Kant's vision. To share that vision is to see the world transformed; to acquire it cannot be the labour of a single day.

The first draft of this book was written in Prague. I am grateful to Dr Ladislav Hejdánek, not only for the invitation to speak to his seminar on the topic of The Categorical Imperative, but also for the example he has set in obeying it. I have benefited from Ruby Meager, Mark Platts and Dorothy Edgington, who commented on a later draft, and from the students of London University who have, over the last decade, made the teaching of Kant's philosophy so rewarding. I have also benefited, in more ways than I can express, from the kindness of Lenka Dvořáková, to whom this book is dedicated.

London, May 1981

Contents

Abbreviations

Quotations are mostly from the English translations referred to below. However, where these translations have seemed to me to be misleading or inelegant, I have used my own.

A   *Critique of Pure Reason*, First Edition, tr. N.Kemp-Smith

B   *Critique of Pure Reason*, Second Edition, tr. N. Kemp-Smith

P   *Critique of Practical Reason*, tr. T. K. Abbott

J   *Critique of Aesthetic Judgement*, tr. J. C. Meredith

T   *Critique of Teleological Judgement*, tr. J. C. Meredith

F   *Foundations of the Metaphysic of Morals*, tr. T. K. Abbott

For the editions of the above works referred to, see notes on further reading.

I   'Inaugural Dissertation', contained in G. B. Kerferd, D. K. E. Walford, and P. G. Lucas (eds): *Kant: Selected Pre-Critical Writings* (Manchester, 1968)

K   *The Kant-Eberhard Controversy*, by H. E. Allison (Baltimore and London, 1973)

L   *Lectures on Ethics*, tr. L. Infield, new edition (New York, 1963)

M   *Prolegomena to any Future Metaphysics*, tr. P. G. Lucas (Manchester, 1953)

C   *Kant's Philosophical Correspondence: 1759–99* ed. and tr. Arnulf Zweig (Chicago, 1967)

All italics that appear in quotations from Kant are his own.

1 Life, works and character

The greatest modern philosopher was moved by nothing more than by duty. His life, in consequence, was unremarkable. For Kant, the virtuous man is so much the master of his passions as scarcely to be prompted by them, and so far indifferent to power and reputation as to regard their significance as nothing beside that of duty itself. Having confined his life so that he could act without strain according to this ideal, Kant devoted himself to scholarship, entirely governed by congenial routines. The little professor of Königsberg has thus become the type of the modern philosopher: bounded in a nutshell, and counting himself king of infinite space.

Immanuel Kant was born in Königsberg in 1724, the fourth of the nine children of a poor harness-maker. Kant's parents were simple people and devout pietists. At that time, pietism, a reformist movement within the Lutheran Church, held powerful sway among the lower and middle classes in Germany, consoling hardship with the idea of the sacredness of work, duty and prayer; its vision of the sovereignty of conscience was to exert a lasting influence on Kant's moral thinking. Although in some respects anti-intellectual, it was also one of the major forces behind the spread of education in late seventeenth-century Germany, and a pietist school had been established in Königsberg. To this school Kant, whose talents had been recognised by a wise and benevolent pastor, was sent at the age of eight. It is fortunate for posterity that such an education should have been offered to one of Kant's lowly origins; it was perhaps less fortunate for the young Kant himself, whose gratitude towards his tutors was so mingled with distaste for their oppressive zeal that in later years he forbore all mention of his early schooling. Some impression of its nature can be gathered from a remark in the little treatise on education, edited from Kant's lecture notes late in his life:

Many people imagine that the years of their youth are the pleasantest and best of their lives; but it is not really so. They are the most troublesome; for we are then under strict discipline, can seldom choose our friends, and still more seldom have our freedom.

In a letter sent to Kant by a former schoolfriend, at a time when both had become famous, the philologist David Ruhnken remarked: 'thirty years have passed since the two of us groaned beneath the pedantically gloomy, but not entirely worthless, discipline of those fanatics'. And it is undeniable that Kant emerged from his schooling with a considerable weight of gloom, together with a remarkable self-discipline. His early manhood was partly devoted to using the second to overcome the first. In this he was almost completely successful. Despite straitened circumstances, a deformed and diminutive body, and the loss both of a father whom he respected and of a mother whom he deeply loved, Kant soon became one of the most popular citizens of Königsberg, welcomed everywhere for his grace, wit and ready conversation.

Kant entered the university of his native city at the age of sixteen and graduated from it six years later. Being unable to secure an academic position, he took work as a private tutor in various households. It was not until the age of thirty-one that he obtained a post at the university, as private docent, an unsalaried employment which conferred the privilege of giving public lectures, and the chance of securing a meagre reward through private tuition. By then Kant had already published works on dynamics and mathematics. He had also acquired, through the connections which his position as private tutor made available, the social ease which was to earn him the title of *der schöne Magister*.

Königsberg was then a city of some dignity, with 50,000 inhabitants and an important garrison. As a seaport serving the trading interests of Eastern Prussia it contained a bustling and variegated population, including Dutch, English, Poles and

Russians. The university, founded in 1544 as the Collegium Albertinum, was a cultural centre of some importance, although so much sunk in provincial obscurity by the mid-eighteenth century that Frederick the Great, visiting the city as crown prince in 1739, described it as 'better suited to the training of bears than to becoming a theatre of the sciences'. Frederick ascended the throne the following year, and did his best to spread into this corner of his kingdom the high culture and intellectual toleration which characterised his reign. Kant, who had already determined to value truth and duty above all things, was therefore fortunate to find that his university offered no major impediments to the pursuit of either. It was perhaps this, as much as his passionate attachment to his birth-place, that prompted him to wait so long for his first appointment, and to continue waiting thereafter, for another fifteen years, before being granted the professorship which he desired. During this period Kant several times refused offers from other German universities, and continued conscientiously to deliver, in the house where he lodged, the lectures which established his reputation. His intellectual labours were devoted mainly to mathematics and physics, and at the age of thirty-one he published a treatise on the origin of the universe which contained the first formulation of the nebular hypothesis. His duties required him, however, to lecture on a wide variety of subjects, including physical geography, about which he became, perhaps because of his reluctance to travel, an acknowledged authority and, in the opinion of one Count Purgstall (who admired the philosopher greatly), a conversational bore.

It is to some extent by chance that Kant's professorship was in metaphysics and logic, rather than in mathematics or natural science. From this point in his career, however, Kant devoted his energies entirely to philosophy, rehearsing in his lectures the thoughts which he was to publish, ten years later, in works which earned him a reputation as the greatest luminary in Germany. The philosopher J. G. Hamann records that it was necessary to arrive in Kant's lecture room at six in the morning, one hour before the professor was due to appear, in order to obtain a place, and Kant's pupil Jachmann has this to say of the performance:

> Kant had a peculiarly skilful method of asserting and defining metaphysical concepts, which consisted, to all appearances, in carrying out his inquiries in front of his audience; as though he himself had just begun to consider the question, gradually adding fresh determining concepts, improving bit by bit on previously established explanations, and finally arriving at a definitive conclusion of his treatment of the subject, which he had thoroughly examined from every angle, having given the completely attentive listener not only a knowledge of the subject, but also an object lesson in methodical thought . . .

And in a letter to a friend, the same writer speaks of Kant's lectures on ethics:

> In these he ceased to be merely a speculative philosopher and became, at the same time, a spirited orator, sweeping the heart and emotions along with him, as well as satisfying the intelligence. Indeed, it was a heavenly delight to hear his sublimely pure ethical doctrine delivered with such powerful philosophic eloquence from the lips of its very creator. How often he moved us to tears, how often he stirred our hearts to their depths, how often he lifted up our minds and emotions from the shackles of self-seeking egoism to the exalted self-awareness of pure free-will, to absolute obedience to the laws of reason and to the exalted sense of our duty to others!

Jachmann is more fulsome than false, and Kant's fame as a speaker, both in private and in public, earned him wide recognition, long before the publication of his greatest works.

Kant's private life is often parodied as one of clockwork routine, fastidious, donnish and self-centred. It is said (because Heine said it) that the housewives of Königsberg would set their clocks by his time of passing; it is said (because Kant once said it) that his constant concern for his bodily condition displayed a morbid hypochondria; it is also said that the bareness of his house and furnishings displayed an indifference to beauty, and that the punctuality of his routine disguised a cold and even frozen heart.

It is true that Kant's life was, if not mechanical, at least highly disciplined. His manservant had instructions to wake him each morning at five and to tolerate no malingering. He would work until seven at his desk, dressed in nightcap and robe, changing back into these garments at once when he had returned from his morning lectures. He remained in his study until one, when he took his single meal of the day, following it, irrespective of the weather, by a walk. He took this exercise alone, from the eccentric conviction that conversation, since it causes a man to breathe through the mouth, should not take place in the open air. He was averse to noise, twice changing lodging in order to avoid the sound of other people, and once writing indignantly to the director of police, commanding him to prevent the inmates of a nearby prison from consoling themselves with the singing of hymns. His aversion to music other than military marches was indeed notorious, as was his total indifference to the visual arts – he possessed only one engraving, a portrait of Rousseau, given to him by a friend.

Kant was aware of the accusations which the intellect draws to itself. And it was to the subject of this engraving that he turned in self-justification, saying that he should have regarded himself as much more worthless than the common labourer, had not Rousseau convinced him that the intellect could play its part in restoring the rights of man. Like all people given to the life of the mind, Kant was in need of the discipline which he imposed on himself. Far from crippling his moral nature, his routine enabled him to flower in the ways best suited to his genius. His love of solitude was balanced by an equal love of company. He would invariably have guests at his midday meal, inviting them on the same morning lest they should be embarrassed by the need to refuse some other invitation, and providing for each a pint of claret, and, if possible, some favourite dish. He conversed, to the delight and instruction of his companions, until three, endeavouring to end the meal in laughter (as much, however, from a conviction that laughter promotes digestion, as from any natural inclination towards it). Kant's writings contain many flashes of satire, and satire, indeed, was his favourite reading. His indifference to music and painting must be set against his love of poetry; even his concern for his health was little more than a consequence of the Kantian philosophy of duty. He neither admired nor enjoyed the sedentary life, but regarded it, nevertheless, as indispensable to the exercise of his intellect. Herder, one of the greatest and most passionate writers of the romantic movement, attended Kant's lectures and afterwards vigorously opposed their influence. He nevertheless thought highly of Kant himself, and summarised his character in these words:

> I had the good fortune to make the acquaintance of a philosopher, who was my teacher. Though in the prime of life, he still had the joyful high spirits of a young man, which he kept, I believe, into extreme old age. His open brow, built for thought, was the seat of indestructible serenity and gladness. A wealth of ideas issued from his lips, jest and wit and good humour were at his bidding, and his instructional lecture was also the most fascinating entertainment.
>
> With the same spirit with which he examined Leibniz, Wolff, Baumgarten, Crusius and Hume, and analysed the laws of nature expounded by the physicists Kepler and Newton, he appraised the currently appearing writings of Rousseau, his *Émile* and his *Héloise*, as he did every fresh discovery in natural science which came to his notice, estimated their value and returned, as always, to an unbiased knowledge of nature and of the moral worth of man.
>
> The history of mankind, of nations and of nature, natural science, mathematics and his own experience were the wellsprings which animated his lectures and his everyday life. He was never indifferent to anything worth knowing. No intrigue, no sectional interests, no advantage, no desire for fame

ever possessed thę slightest power to counteract his extension and illumination of truth. He encouraged and gently compelled people to think for themselves: despotism was alien to his nature. This man, whom I name with the deepest gratitude and reverence, is Immanuel Kant; I recall his image with pleasure.

Kant's duties as a university teacher required him to lecture on all aspects of philosophy, and for many years he devoted the major part of his intellectual efforts to teaching, publishing short and undeveloped books and papers. His greatest achievement – the *Critique of Pure Reason* – was also his first major publication, appearing in 1781, when Kant was fifty-seven. Of this work he wrote to Moses Mendelssohn 'although the book is the product of twelve years of reflection, I completed it hastily, in perhaps four or five months, with the greatest attentiveness to its content but less care about its style and ease of comprehension' (C 105–6). In an attempt to alleviate the difficulties presented by the *Critique* he published a short *Prolegomena to any Future Metaphysic which shall lay Claim to being a Science* (1783), in which brilliant polemic is combined with an obscure condensation of the *Critique*'s most offending passages. For the second edition of the *Critique*, in 1787, Kant rewrote the most forbidding sections; since the result is equally difficult, commentators have come to agree that the opacity of Kant's work stems not so much from the style as from the thought itself. Despite its difficulty, however, the work rapidly became so famous that the 'critical philosophy' was being advocated, taught, opposed, and sometimes even censored and persecuted, throughout the German-speaking world. Kant's self-confidence increased, and he was able to write in 1787 to K. L. Rheinhold (who did much to popularise Kant's ideas): 'I can assure you that the longer I continue in my path the less worried I become that any contradiction . . . will ever significantly damage my system' (C 127). The influence of Kant's first *Critique* is justly summarised by Mme de Staël, when, thirty years after the first edition, she wrote that 'when at length the treasures of thought which it contains were discovered, it produced such a sensation in Germany, that almost all which has been accomplished since, in literature as well as in philosophy, has flowed from the impulse given by this performance'.

During the twelve years of reflection to which Kant refers in his letter to Mendelssohn he published almost nothing, and his earlier ('pre-critical') writings are of peripheral interest to the student of his mature philosophy. However, once the critical philosophy had achieved expression, Kant continued, with increasing confidence, to explore its ramifications. The *Critique of Pure Reason* dealt in a systematic way with metaphysics and the theory of knowledge; it was followed by the *Critique of Practical Reason* (1788), concerned with ethics, and the *Critique of Judgement* (1790), concerned largely with aesthetics. Many other works were added to those, and Kant's collected writings in the so-called *Berliner Ausgabe* now fill twenty-seven volumes. Of these other works, two will particularly concern us: the *Prolegomena*, already mentioned, and the *Foundations of the Metaphysic of Morals*, which appeared in 1785, before the second *Critique*, and contains a compelling expression of Kant's moral theory.

During the reign of Frederick the Great Königsberg breathed the air of enlightenment, and Kant enjoyed the esteem of Frederick's ministers, in particular of von Zedlitz, the minister of education, to whom the *Critique of Pure Reason* is dedicated. A marked change occurred when Frederick William II ascended the throne. His minister, Woellner, exerted great influence, and, becoming responsible for religion in 1788, attempted to bring religious toleration to an end. Kant's *Religion Within the Limits of Reason Alone* was published in 1793, under the imprint of the Königsberg philosophy faculty, thus escaping censorship on a point of law. Woellner, mightily displeased, wrote in the King's name to Kant, charging him to give an account of himself. Kant replied with a solemn promise to his sovereign not to engage in public discussion of religion, either through lectures or through writings. Kant regarded himself as absolved from this promise by the monarch's death. Nevertheless this conflict with authority caused him much pain and bitterness. Kant prided himself on being a loyal subject, despite republican sympathies which he once expressed in the presence of an Englishman with such vivacity as to call forth a challenge to a duel, and with such eloquence as to overcome both the challenge and the opinions of the man who had offered it. (The man in question, Joseph Green, was a merchant in Königsberg, and subsequently became Kant's closest friend.)

Kant enjoyed the company of women (provided that they did not pretend to understand the *Critique of Pure Reason*) and twice contemplated marriage. On each occasion, however, he hesitated long enough to ensure that he remained unwed. One day, his disreputable and drunken manservant appeared at table in a yellow coat. Kant indignantly ordered him to take it off and sell it, promising to make good the financial loss. He then learned with amazement that the servant had been married, was a widower, and was now to marry again, the yellow coat having been purchased for the occasion. Kant was appalled at these revelations, and never again looked on his servant with favour. It seems that he was unable to persuade himself of the normality of marriage, which he once described as an agreement between two people for the 'reciprocal use of each other's sexual organs' (C 235). However, in his early *Observations on the Sentiment of the Beautiful and the Sublime* (1764), Kant had written eloquently on the distinction between the sexes. He was radically opposed to the view that men and women partake of a common nature which alone suffices to determine the character of their relations; instead, he assigned to women a charm, beauty, and capacity to melt the heart which are foreign to the more 'sublime', 'principled' and 'practical' sex to which he belonged. This description of women accords with Kant's description of natural beauty. It was nature, above all, that stirred his emotions, and it was to scenes of natural beauty that his mother had taken him as a child, so as to awaken his feelings towards the things she loved. It is possible to discern in his evocations, both of feminine charm, and of natural beauty, the residue of erotic feelings which, had they been more actively expressed, might well have broken the routine to which our intellectual history is so heavily indebted.

Kant gave his last official lecture in 1796. By that time his faculties had begun to decline and a sombre melancholy had replaced his former gaiety. Fichte describes him as seeming to lecture in his sleep, waking with a start to his half-forgotten subject-matter. Soon he lost his clarity of mind, his ability to recognise old friends, even his ability to complete simple sentences. He faded into insensibility, and passed from his blameless life on 12 February 1804, unaccompanied by his former intellectual powers. He was attended to his grave by people from all over Germany, and by the whole of Königsberg, being acknowleged even in his senility as the greatest glory of that town. His grave crumbled away and was restored in 1881. His remains were moved in 1924, to a solemn neo-classical portico attached to the cathedral. In 1950 unknown vandals broke open the sarcophagus, and left it empty. By that time Königsberg had ceased to be a centre of learning, had been absorbed into the Soviet Union, and had been renamed in honour of one of the few of Stalin's henchmen to die of natural causes. A bronze tablet remains fixed to the wall of the Castle, overlooking the dead and wasted city, bearing these words from the concluding section of the *Critique of Practical Reason*:

Two things fill the heart with ever renewed and increasing awe and reverence, the more often and the more steadily we meditate upon them: *the starry firmament above and the moral law within.*

It is fortunate for the inhabitants of Kaliningrad that they are daily reminded of two things that they may still admire.

2 The background of Kant's thought

The *Critique of Pure Reason* is the most important work of philosophy to have been written in modern times; it is also one of the most difficult. It poses questions so novel and comprehensive that Kant judged it necessary to invent technical terms with which to discuss them. These terms have a strange beauty and compellingness, and it is impossible to acquire a full appreciation of Kant's work without experiencing the order and connectedness that his vocabulary imposes upon the traditional problems of philosophy. Nevertheless, the gist of Kant's thought can be expressed in a lowlier idiom, and in what follows I shall try to eliminate as many of his technicalities as I can. The task is not easy, since there is no accepted interpretation of their meaning. While a 'picture' of the Kantian system is common to all who have commented on it, there is no agreement whatsoever as to the strength, or even as to the content, of his arguments. A commentator who presents clear premises and clear conclusions will invariably be accused of missing Kant's argument, and the only way to escape academic censure is to fall into the verbal mannerisms of the original. It has become, in recent years, slightly easier to risk this censure. Contemporary Kantian studies – in particular in Britain and America – have tended to the view that the obscurity of Kantian scholarship is often a product of its confusion. In order not to attribute the confusion to Kant, scholars have laboured hard to elicit from, or at least to impose upon, the first *Critique*, an interpretation that renders it intelligible. I shall try to do the same, and shall be more influenced by these contemporary studies than I am able to acknowledge.

The first problem posed by the interpretation of the *Critique of Pure Reason* is this: what are the questions which it hopes to answer? Kant wrote, in the preface to the first edition:

In this enquiry I have made completeness my aim, and I ven-
ture to assert that there is not a single metaphysical problem
which has not been solved, or for the solution of which the
key at least has not been supplied. (A xiii)

While this represents the ambition, if not the achievement, of
the first *Critique*, Kant was in fact motivated by more specific
interests. If we turn to the historical antecedents of Kant's argument, we can extract from the philosophical controversies
which influenced him certain major subjects of dispute. The
most important we find to be the problem of objective knowledge, as this had been posed by Descartes. I can know much
about myself, and this knowledge often has a character of certainty. In particular it is senseless, according to Descartes, to
doubt that I exist. Here, doubt only confirms what is doubted.
Cogito ergo sum. In this case, at least, I have objective knowledge. The fact that I exist is an objective fact; it is a fact about
the world and not just about someone's perception. Whatever
the world contains, it contains the thinking being who I am.
Kant's contemporary Lichtenberg pointed out that Descartes
ought not to have drawn this conclusion. The 'cogito' shows
that there is a thought, but not that there is an 'I' who thinks it.
Kant, similarly dissatisfied with Descartes's argument, and with
the doctrine of the soul that flowed from it, felt that the certainty of self-knowledge had been wrongly described. It is true that,
however sceptical I may be about the world, I cannot extend my
scepticism into the subjective sphere (the sphere of consciousness): so I can be immediately certain of my present mental
states. But I cannot be immediately certain of what I am, or of
whether, indeed, there is an 'I' to whom these states belong.
These further propositions must be established by argument,
and that argument had yet to be found.

What is the character of this immediate and certain knowledge? The distinguishing feature of my present mental states is
that they are as they seem to me and seem as they are. In the
subjective sphere being and seeming collapse into each other. In
the objective sphere they diverge. The world is objective be-

cause it can be other than it seems to me. So the true question of objective knowledge is: how can I know the world as it is? I can have knowledge of the world as it *seems*, since that is merely knowledge of my present perceptions, memories, thoughts and feelings. But can I have knowledge of the world that is *not* just knowledge of how it seems? To put the question in slightly more general form: can I have knowledge of the world which is not just knowledge of my own point of view? Science, common sense, theology and personal life all suppose the possibility of objective knowledge. If this supposition is unwarranted then so are almost all the beliefs that we commonly entertain.

Among Kant's immediate predecessors two in particular had provided answers to the question of objectivity which were sufficiently decisive to command the attention of the intellectual world. These were G. W. Leibniz (1646–1716) and David Hume (1711–76); the first claimed that we could have objective knowledge of the world uncontaminated by the point of view of any observer, the second claimed (or at least seemed to his contemporaries to claim) that we could have objective knowledge of nothing.

Leibniz was the founding father of Prussian academic philosophy. His thought, left to the world in succinct and unpublished fragments, had been built into a system by Christian von Wolff (1679–1754), and applied and extended by Wolff's pupil, the former pietist, A. G. Baumgarten (1714–62). The Leibnizian system had met with official censure during Kant's youth, since it made such claims for reason as to threaten those of faith; for a time Wolff was forbidden to teach. But the system was restored to favour under Frederick the Great, and became the orthodox metaphysics of the German Enlightenment. Kant respected this orthodoxy, and to the end of his days would use Baumgarten's works as texts for his lectures. But Hume's scepticism made a deep impression on him, and introduced new problems which he felt could be answered only by overthrowing the Leibnizian system. These problems, concerning causality and a priori knowledge (i.e. knowledge not based in experience), were combined with the question of objectivity to form the peculiar subject-matter of the first *Critique*.

Leibniz belonged to the school of thought now generally labelled 'rationalist', and Hume to the school of 'empiricism' which is commonly contrasted with it. Kant, believing that both philosophies were wrong in their conclusions, attempted to give an account of philosophical method which incorporated the truths, and avoided the errors, of both. Rationalism derives all knowledge from the exercise of reason, and purports to give an absolute description of the world, uncontaminated by the experience of any observer. Empiricism argues that knowledge comes through experience alone; there is therefore no possibility of separating knowledge from the subjective condition of the knower. Kant wished to give an answer to the question of objective knowledge which was neither as absolute as Leibniz's nor as subjective as Hume's. The best way to make his unique position intelligible is to begin by summarising the two views which he strove to reject.

Leibniz believed that the understanding contains within itself certain innate principles, which it knows intuitively to be true, and which form the axioms from which a complete description of the world can be derived. These principles are necessarily true, and do not depend upon experience for their confirmation. Hence they lead to a description of the world as it is, not as it appears in experience or to a circumscribed 'point of view'. At the same time the 'points of view' which are characteristic of individuals can be fitted into the rational picture of the world. Leibniz recognised a division in thought between subject and predicate; (in the sentence 'John thinks' the subject-term is 'John', and the predicate-term is 'thinks'). He believed that this division corresponds to a distinction in reality between substance and property. The fundamental objects in the world are substances. These, he thought, must be self-dependent, unlike the properties which inhere in them: for example, a substance can exist without thinking, but no thinking can exist without a substance. Being self-dependent substances are also indestructible, except by a miracle. He called them 'monads', and his model for the monad was the individual soul, the thinking substance, as this had been described by Descartes. From this idea, he derived his 'perspectiveless' picture of the world, relying on two fundamental laws of reason: the Principle of Contradiction (a proposition and its negation cannot both be true), and the Principle of Sufficient Reason (nothing is true which has no sufficient explanation). By means of ingenious and subtle arguments and making the fewest possible assumptions, he arrived at the following conclusions.

The world consists of infinitely many individual monads which exist neither in space nor in time, but eternally. Each monad is different in some respect from every other (the famous 'identity of indiscernibles'). Without that assumption objects cannot be individuated in terms of their intrinsic properties; a point of view then becomes necessary from which to tell things apart, and it is Leibniz's contention that the real nature of the world can be given from no point of view. The point of view of each monad is simply a way of representing its internal constitution; it does not represent the world as it is in itself. Each monad mirrors the universe from its own point of view, but no monad can enter into real relation, causal or otherwise, with any other. Even space and time are intellectual constructs, through which we make our experience intelligible, but which do not belong to the world as such. However, by the principle of 'pre-established harmony', the successive properties of every monad correspond to the successive properties of every other. So we can describe our successive states of mind as 'perceptions', and the world will 'appear' to each monad in a way which corresponds to its appearance to every other. There is a system among appearances, and within this system it makes sense to speak of spatial, temporal and causal relations; of destructible individuals and dynamic principles; of perception, activity and influence. These ideas, and the physical laws which we derive from them, depend for their validity on the underlying harmony among points of view which they describe. They do not yield knowledge of the real world of monads except indirectly, on account of our assurance that the way things appear bears the metaphysical imprint of the way things are. When two watches keep exact time together I might be tempted to think that the one causes the other to move. This is an example of a merely apparent relation. In some such way Leibniz argued that the whole world of common-sense belief and perception is no more than an appearance or 'phenomenon'. But it is, Leibniz said, a 'well-founded' phenomenon. It is no illusion, but a necessary and systematic offshoot of the operation of those rational principles which determine how things really are. The real substances, because they are described and identified from no point of view, are without phenomenal characteristics. Reality itself is accessible to reason alone, since only reason can rise above the individual point of view and participate in the vision of ultimate necessities, which is also God's. Hence reason must operate through 'innate' ideas. These are ideas which have been acquired through no experience and which belong to all thinking beings. They owe their content not to experience but to the intuitive capacities of reason. Among these ideas is that of substance, from which all Leibniz's principles ultimately flow.

Hume's vision is in some measure the opposite of Leibniz's. He denies the possibility of knowledge through reason, since reason cannot operate without ideas, and ideas are acquired only through the senses. The content of every thought must be given, in the last analysis, in terms of the experiences which warrant it, and no belief can be established as true except by reference to the sensory 'impressions' which provide its guarantee. (This is the general assumption of empiricism.) But the only experience that can confirm anything for *me* is *my* experience. The testimony of others, or of records, the formulation of laws or hypotheses, the appeal to memory and induction – all these depend for their authority on the experiences which guarantee them. My experiences are as they seem, and seem as they are, for here 'seeming' is all that there is. Hence there is no problem as to how I can know them. But in basing all knowledge on experience Hume reduces my knowledge of the world to knowledge of my point of view. All claims to objectivity become spurious and illusory. When I claim to have knowledge of objects existing externally to my perceptions, all I can really mean is that those perceptions exhibit a kind of constancy and coherence which generates the (illusory) idea of independence. When I refer to causal necessities all I am entitled to mean is the regular succession among experiences, together with the subjective sense of anticipation which arises from that. As for reason, this can tell us of the 'relations of ideas': for example, it can tell us that the idea of space is included in that of shape, or that the idea of a bachelor is identical with that of an unmarried man. But it can neither generate ideas of its own, nor decide whether an idea has application. It is the source only of trivial knowledge derived from the meanings of words; it can never lead to knowledge of matters of fact. Hume took his scepticism so far as to cast doubt upon the existence of the self (that entity which had provided the model for Leibniz's monad), saying that neither is there a perceivable object that goes by this name, nor is there any experience that would give rise to the idea of it.

Such scepticism, reaching back into that very point of view from which scepticism begins, is intolerable, and it is not surprising that Kant was, as he put it, aroused by Hume from 'dogmatic slumbers' (M 9). The parts of Hume's philosophy which most disturbed him concerned the concept of causality. Hume had argued that there is no foundation for the belief in necessities in nature: necessity belongs to thought alone, and merely reflects the 'relations of ideas'. It was this that led Kant to perceive that natural science rests on the belief that there are real necessities, so that Hume's scepticism, far from being an academic exercise, threatened to undermine the foundations of scientific thought. Kant did indeed have a lasting quarrel with Leibniz, and with the Leibnizian system. But it was the sense that the problems of objectivity and of causal necessity are ultimately connected that led him towards the outlook of the *Critique of Pure Reason*. It was only then that he perceived what was really wrong with Leibniz, through his attempt to show what was really wrong with Hume. He came to think as follows.

Neither experience nor reason are alone able to provide knowledge. The first provides content without form, the second form without content. Only in their synthesis is knowledge possible; hence there is no knowledge that does not bear the marks of reason and of experience together. Such knowledge is, however, genuine and objective. It transcends the point of view of the man who possesses it, and makes legitimate claims about an independent world. Nevertheless, it is impossible to know the world 'as it is in itself', independent of all perspective. Such an absolute conception of the object of knowledge is senseless, Kant argues, since it can be given only by employing concepts from which every element of meaning has been refined away. While I can know the world independently of my point of view on it, what I know (the world of 'appearance') bears the indelible marks of that point of view. Objects do not depend for their existence upon my perceiving them; but their nature is determined by the fact that they *can* be perceived. Objects are not Leibnizian monads, knowable only to the perspectiveless stance of 'pure reason'; nor are they Humean 'impressions', features of my own experience. They are objective, but their character is given by the point of view through which they can be known. This is the point of view of 'possible experience'. Kant tries to show that, properly understood, the idea of 'experience' already carries the objective reference which Hume denied. Experience contains *within* itself the features of space, time and causality. Hence in describing my experience I am referring to an ordered perspective on an independent world.

In order to introduce this novel conception of objectivity (to which he gave the name 'transcendental idealism') Kant began from an exploration of a priori knowledge. Among true propositions, some are true independently of experience, and remain true however experience varies: these are the a priori truths. Others owe their truth to experience, and might have been false had experience been different: these are the a posteriori truths. (The terminology here was not invented by Kant, although it owes its popularity to Kant's frequent use of it.) Kant argued that a priori truths are of two kinds, which he called 'analytic' and 'synthetic' (A 6–10). An analytic truth is one like 'All bachelors are unmarried' whose truth is guaranteed by the meaning, and discovered through the analysis, of the terms used to express it. A synthetic truth is one whose truth is not so derived but which, as Kant puts it, affirms something in the predicate which is not already contained in the subject. It is a truth like 'All bachelors are unfulfilled' which (supposing it to be true) says something substantial about bachelors and does not merely reiterate the definition of the term used to refer to them. The distinction between the analytic and the synthetic involved novel terminology, although similar distinctions can be found in earlier philosophers. Aquinas, inspired by Boethius, defines a 'self-evident' proposition as one in which the 'predicate is contained in the notion of the subject', and a similar idea is to be found in Leibniz. What is original, however, is Kant's insistence that the two distinctions (between the a priori and the a posteriori, and between the analytic and the synthetic), are of a wholly different nature. It is mere dogmatism on the part of empiricists to think that they must coincide. And yet for the empiricist view to be true, there cannot be synthetic a priori knowledge: synthetic truths can be known only through experience.

The empiricist position has been taken in our time by the logical positivists of the 'Vienna circle', who argued that all a priori truths are analytic, and drew the conclusion that any metaphysical proposition must be meaningless, since it could be neither analytic nor a posteriori. It was already apparent to Kant that empiricism denies the possibility of metaphysics. And yet metaphysics is necessary if foundations are to be provided for objective knowledge: without it, there is no conceivable barrier against the scepticism of Hume. So the first question of all philosophy becomes 'How is synthetic a priori knowledge possible?' Or, to put it another way, 'How can I come to know the world through pure reflection, without recourse to experience?' Kant felt that there could be no explanation of a priori knowledge which divorces the object known from the perspective of the knower. Hence he was sceptical of all attempts to claim that we can have a priori knowledge of some timeless, spaceless world of the 'thing-in-itself' (any object defined without reference to the 'possible experience' of an observer). I can have a priori knowledge only of the world that I experience. A priori knowledge provides support for, but it also derives its content from, empirical discovery. Kant's *Critique* is directed against the assumption that 'pure reason' can give content to knowledge without making reference to experience.

All a priori truths are both necessary and absolutely universal: these are the two signs whereby we can discern, among our claims to knowledge, those items which, if they are true at all, are true a priori. For it is obvious that experience could never confer necessity or absolute universality on anything; any experience *might* have been otherwise, and experience is necessarily finite and particular, so that a universal law (which has indefinitely many instances) could never be truly confirmed by it. No one should really doubt that there is synthetic a priori knowledge: Kant gave as the most conspicuous example mathematics, which we know by pure reasoning, but not by analysing the meanings of mathematical terms. There ought to be a philosophical explanation of the a priori nature of mathematics, and Kant attempted to provide it in the opening sections of the *Critique*. But he also drew attention to other examples, of a more puzzling kind. For instance, the following propositions seem to be true a priori: 'Every event has a cause'; 'The world consists of enduring objects which exist independently of me'; 'All discoverable objects are in space and time.' These propositions cannot be established through experience, since their truth is presupposed in the interpretation of experience. Moreover, each claims to be true, not just on this or that occasion, but universally and necessarily. Finally, it is just such truths as these that are required for the proof of objectivity. Hence the problem of objectivity and the problem of synthetic a priori knowledge are ultimately connected. Moreover, the vital role played by the truths given above in all scientific explanation persuaded Kant that a theory of objectivity would also provide an explanation of natural necessity. Such a theory would then give a complete answer to the scepticism of Hume.

What, then, are Kant's aims in the first *Critique*? First, in opposition to Hume, to show that synthetic a priori knowledge is possible, and to offer examples of it. Secondly, in opposition to Leibniz, to demonstrate that 'pure reason' alone, operating outside the constraints placed on it by experience, leads only to illusion, so that there is no a priori knowledge of 'things-in-themselves'. It is normal to divide the *Critique* into two parts, in accordance with this division of the subject, and to describe the first part as the 'Analytic', the second as the 'Dialectic'. While this division does not correspond exactly to Kant's division of chapters (which is exceedingly complex and bristles with technicalities), it is sufficiently close not to be misleading. The terms 'analytic' and 'dialectic' are Kant's: and so is the bifurcation of the argument. In the first part Kant's defence of objectivity is expounded, and it is with the argument of the 'Analytic' that I shall begin, for until it is grasped, it will be impossible to understand the nature either of Kant's metaphysics, or of the moral and aesthetic doctrines which he later brought within its purview.

3 The transcendental deduction

Kant's answer to the fundamental question of metaphysics – 'How is synthetic a priori knowledge possible?' – contains two parts. I shall call these, following Kant's own terminology (A xvi), the 'subjective' and the 'objective' deductions. The first had been partly adumbrated in Kant's inaugural dissertation of 1770 (I 54ff.), and consists in a theory of cognition. It tries to show what is involved in making a judgement: in holding something to be true or false. It concentrates on the nature of the mind, in particular on the nature of belief, sensation and experience. Its conclusions are presented as part of a general theory of the 'understanding' (the faculty of judgement). Kant repeatedly emphasises that the theory is not to be construed as empirical psychology. It is not, nor does it purport to be, a theory of the workings of the *human*, as opposed to some other, intelligence. It is a theory of the understanding as such, telling us what it is, and how it must function if there are to be judgements at all. In all philosophical discussion of these matters, Kant argues, we are talking 'not about the origin of experience, but about what lies in it' (M 63). And he compares such purely philosophical questions to that 'analysis of concepts' which has since become so fashionable. Kant wishes to draw the limits of the understanding. If there are things which cannot be grasped by the understanding, then all assertions about them are meaningless.

The objective deduction consists in a positive attempt to establish the content of a priori knowledge. The argument here proceeds, not by an analysis of the faculties of knowledge, but by an exploration of its grounds. What are the presuppositions of experience? What has to be true if we are to have even that bare point of view which the sceptics ascribe to us? If we can identify these presuppositions, then they will be established as true a priori. For their truth follows, not from the fact that we have this or that experience, but from the fact that we have experience *at all*. Hence they depend upon no particular experience for their verification, and can be established by reasoning alone. They will be true in every world where the sceptical question can be asked (in every comprehensible world). And this is tantamount to their being necessary. I cannot conceive of their falsehood, since I cannot conceive *myself* as part of a world which refutes them.

Kant calls this argument the 'transcendental deduction', and the resulting theory 'transcendental idealism'. The word 'transcendental' needs some explanation. An argument is transcendental if it 'transcends' the limits of empirical enquiry, so as to establish the a priori conditions of experience. We must distinguish transcendental from empirical argument (B 81); the former, unlike the latter, leads to 'knowledge which is occupied not so much with objects as with the mode of our knowledge of objects *in so far as this mode of knowledge is possible a priori*' (B 25). The word 'transcendental' is also used by Kant in another sense, to refer to 'transcendental objects'. These are objects which transcend experience, i.e. which are not disclosed to empirical investigation, being neither observable themselves, nor causally related to what is observable. These 'transcendental objects' present a problem of interpretation to which I shall return in Chapter 4.

I shall also return to the interpretation of 'transcendental idealism'. Briefly, this theory implies that the laws of the understanding, laid down in the subjective deduction, are the same as the a priori truths established in the objective deduction. It implies, in other words, a very special kind of harmony between the capacities of the knower and the nature of the known. It is because of this harmony that a priori knowledge is possible.

It follows from this theory that the 'forms of thought' which govern the understanding, and the a priori nature of reality, are in exact correspondence. The world is as we think it, and we think it as it is. Almost all the major difficulties in the interpretation of Kant depend upon which of those two propositions is emphasised. Is it our thought which determines the a priori nature of the world? Or is it the world which determines how we must think of it? The answer, I believe, is 'neither, and both'. But only at the very end of this essay will that answer be clear.

Self-consciousness

I have referred, adopting Kant's usage, to 'our' understanding and experience. Who are 'we'? Kant's use of the first person plural is a device of a very special character. He is not, as I said, engaging in a psychological study of 'creatures like us'. Nor is he speaking with some abstract authorial voice for which no true subject can be found. He means the term 'we' to denote indifferently any being who can use the term 'I': anyone who can identify *himself* as the subject of experience. The starting-point of all Kant's philosophy is the single premise of self-consciousness, and his three *Critiques* concern themselves respectively with the questions: 'What must a self-conscious being think?', 'What must he do?' and 'What must he find agreeable?' Self-consciousness is a deep phenomenon, with many layers and aspects: different features of it are invoked as we tackle each of those questions. In the case of the first *Critique* the feature is that which Kant regarded as providing common ground between himself and the empiricists whom he sought to refute: self-conscious experience. It is not every being that can know his own experience (for whom the 'I think' can accompany all his perceptions, as Kant expresses his crucial emendation of Descartes (B 131–2)). But it is only such a being who can pose the sceptical question: 'Are things as they seem to me (as my experience represents them)?' The argument explores, therefore, the presuppositions of this self-consciousness. Kant's conclusion can be summarised thus: the conditions which make scepticism possible also show that it is false.

The transcendental synthesis

I shall deal first with the subjective deduction – the theory of the 'subjective conditions' of judgement. There are two sources from which our knowledge is drawn: sensibility and understanding. The first is a faculty of intuitions (*Anschauungen*): it includes all the sensory states and modifications which empiricists think to be the sole basis of knowledge. The second is a faculty of concepts. Since concepts have to be *applied* in judgements, this faculty, unlike sensibility, is active. It is a mistake of empiricism, Kant argued, not to have understood this crucial point, and to have construed all concepts of the understanding on the model of sensations. (Thus for Hume a concept is simply a faded relict of the 'impression' from which it derives.) The corresponding mistake of rationalism is to think of sensation as a kind of confused aspiration towards conceptual thought. Thus Kant summarised the famous dispute between Leibniz and Locke in the following way: 'Leibniz *intellectualised* appearances, just as Locke ... *sensualised* the concepts of the understanding'. In fact, however, there are two faculties here, irreducible the one to the other; they 'can supply objectively valid judgements of things only in *conjunction* with each other' (A 271, B 327).

Judgement requires, then, the joint operation of sensibility and understanding. A mind without concepts would have no capacity to think; equally, a mind armed with concepts, but with no sensory data to which they could be applied, would have nothing to think *about*. 'Without sensibility no object would be given to us, without understanding no object would be thought. Thoughts without content are empty; intuitions without concepts are blind' (A 51, B 75). Judgement requires what Kant calls a 'synthesis' of concept and intuition, and only in this synthesis is true experience (as opposed to mere 'intuition') generated. This synthesis is somewhat confusingly described by Kant: sometimes it seems to be a 'process' whereby experience is generated, at other times a kind of 'structure' which experience contains. In any event, it seems to have two stages: the 'pure' synthesis, whereby intuitions are grouped together into a totality, and then the act of judgement, in which the totality is given form through a concept (A 79, B 104). This synthesis is not meant to be a psychological fact; it is a 'transcendental' as opposed to an 'empirical' synthesis. In other words, it is *presupposed* in (self-conscious) experience, and not derived from it. I do not lay hold of my experience and then subject it to synthesis. For the very act of 'laying hold' presupposes that this synthesis has occurred. Suppose I attempt to describe how things seem to me, as I sit writing at this desk. I am at once engaged in the activity of subsuming my sensory awareness under concepts (such concepts as those of desk and writing). I can represent my experience to myself only by describing 'how things seem': and that is to use the concepts of the understanding. Conversely, none of my concepts would be intelligible without the experiences which exhibit their application.

A priori concepts

It is an assumption of empiricism that all concepts are derived from, or in some manner reducible to, the sensory intuitions which warrant their application. There can be no concept without the corresponding sensory stimulus, and it is in terms of such stimulus that the meaning of a concept must be given. Kant argued that this assumption is absurd. The empiricists confuse experience with sensation. Experience can provide the grounds for the application of a concept, because it already contains a concept, in accordance with the 'synthesis' just described. Sensation, or intuition, contains no concept, and provides grounds for no judgement. Until transformed by mental activity, all sensation is without intellectual structure, and therefore provides grounds for no belief. If we understand experiences, then it is because they already contain within themselves the concepts which we supposedly derive from them. Whence came these concepts? Not from the senses. There must therefore be some repertoire of concepts contained within the understanding itself, and which defines the forms of its activity.

It follows that the Leibnizian theory of 'innate ideas' is substantially correct. There are concepts which cannot be given *through* experience because they are presupposed *in* experience. They are involved in every apprehension of the world that I can represent as mine; not to possess them is to have, not experience, but mere intuition, from which no knowledge can be derived. These 'a priori concepts' of the understanding prescribe the basic 'forms' of judgement. All other concepts can be seen as 'determinations' of them – that is, as special cases, more or less adulterated by the reference to observation and experiment.

Kant called these fundamental concepts 'categories', borrowing a term that had been put to similar (but less systematic) use by Aristotle. The categories are our forms of thought. One such category is the concept which lies at the origin of the Leibnizian system: the category of substance. A substance is that which is able to exist independently, and which supports the properties which depend upon it. The concept 'chair' is a special, empirical determination of the general concept of substance. It can be acquired only by someone who already grasps that general concept, for only such a person would be able to interpret his experience in the requisite way. Another category is the one that had been subjected to such sceptical attack by Hume: the category of cause. It is not surprising that much of the argument of the Analytic concerns the ideas of substance and causality, as Kant wished us to understand them. However, he gave a list of twelve categories in all, and found to his satisfaction that they corresponded to all the disputes of traditional metaphysics.

The subjective deduction

It seems to follow from the above account that if we are to have knowledge at all, our intuitions must permit application of the categories. To speak more directly: It must seem to us that we are confronted by substances, causes and the rest. So we can know a priori that every comprehensible world (every world which could contain self-consciousness) must also have the appearance dictated by the categories. It can have that appearance only if it appears to obey certain 'principles'. A principle specifies the conditions under which a category gains application. The sum of all principles defines the extent of our claims to a priori knowledge.

What does this 'subjective deduction' of the categories establish? The answer seems to be this: we must think in terms of the categories, and must therefore accept as true the principles which govern their application. So the world must ordinarily appear to us in such a way that we *can* accept these principles. Self-consciousness requires that the world must appear to 'conform to the categories'. This assertion contains the essence of what Kant called his 'Copernican Revolution' in philosophy. Previous philosophers had taken nature as primary, and asked how our cognitive capacities could lay hold of it. Kant takes those capacities as primary, and then deduces the a priori limits of nature. This is the first important step in his answer to Hume. It is well for Hume to assert that our knowledge has its foundation in experience. But experience is not the simple concept that Hume supposed it to be. Experience contains intellectual structure. It is already organised in accordance with the ideas of space, time, substance and causality. Hence there is no knowledge of experience that does not point towards a world of nature. Our point of view is intrinsically a point of view *on* an objective world.

But does that answer the sceptic? Surely, he will say, even if Kant were right, and the world must appear to us in this way, does it also have to *be* as it *appears*? Even if we are compelled to think that the categories apply, it does not follow that they really *do* apply. We have yet to pass from the description of our point of view to a description of the world. The problem therefore remains, how 'subjective conditions of thought can have objective validity' (A 89, B 122). As Kant argues (B 141), there can be no judgement without objectivity. Clearly then, an 'objective deduction' of the categories is required: an argument that will show that the world, and not just our experience of the world, is in conformity with the a priori principles of the understanding.

Forms of thought and forms of intuition

Before proceeding to that objective deduction we must return to the earlier sections of the *Critique of Pure Reason*, in which Kant writes in general terms about the nature of sensibility. Kant believed that he had arrived at his list of categories by a process of abstraction. Suppose I describe what I now see: a pen writing. The concept 'pen' is a special 'determination' of the wider concept 'artifact', itself a determination of 'material object', and so on. The limit of this train of abstraction is the a priori concept which each stage exemplifies: the concept of substance. Beyond that point we cannot abstract further, without ceasing to think. Likewise 'writing' is a determination of 'action', which is a determination of 'force', and so on: the category here being that of cause or explanation, beyond which the understanding cannot proceed. By these, and similar, thought-experiments, Kant supposed that he had isolated, through his list of the twelve categories, all the forms of judgement, and so given an exposition of the concept of objective truth. Hence the proof of the objectivity of our claims to knowledge involves the demonstration of the 'objective validity' of the categories, and of the principles presupposed in their application.

There are two ideas, however, which, despite their importance to science and to the objective view of the world, are not included in Kant's list of categories. These are the ideas of space and time, which he described, not as concepts, but as forms of intuition. Space and time are discussed in the opening section of the first *Critique*, the 'Transcendental Aesthetic'. The word 'aesthetic' here derives from the Greek for sensation, and indicates that the subject-matter of this section is the faculty of sensibility, considered independently of the understanding. Kant argued that space and time, far from being concepts applicable to intuitions, are basic *forms* of intuition, meaning that every sensation must bear the imprint of temporal, and sometimes of spatial, organisation.

Time is the form of 'inner sense', that is, of all states of mind, whether or not they are referred to an objective reality. There could not be a mental state that is not in time, and time is made real to us through this organisation in our experience. Space is the form of 'outer sense' – that is, of those 'intuitions' which we refer to an independent world and which we therefore regard as 'appearances' of objective things. Nothing can appear to me as independent of myself without also being experienced as 'outside', and therefore as spatially related to myself. Space, like time, forms part of the organisation of my sensibility. My very sense-impressions bear the form of space, as is evidenced in the phenomenon of the 'visual field'.

But why deny that space and time are a priori concepts? They are a priori, but they cannot be concepts, since concepts are general, admitting of a plurality of instances. Kant argued that there is of necessity only one space, and only one time. All spaces form parts of a single space, and all times parts of a single time. Kant sometimes expresses this point by saying that space and time are not concepts but 'a priori intuitions'.

There is, in Kant's philosophy, a rage for order that leads him to attempt to solve as many philosophical questions as possible through each distinct part of his system. One motive for treating space and time separately from the categories of the understanding is in order to suggest an explanation for the fact that there are two kinds of synthetic a priori truth: mathematics and metaphysics. It seems that there ought to be a different explanation for each, since mathematics is self-evident, and obvious to all thinking beings, whereas metaphysics is essentially disputed, a matter over which people argue interminably; 'infinitely removed from being as evident as the proposition that twice two makes four' (A 733, B 761). Mathematics possesses, indeed, all the immediacy and indubitability of intuition itself, whereas the metaphysical principles, which derive from thought alone, are necessarily contentious. By construing mathematics as an a priori science of intuition Kant thought that he could show why this is so. In mathematics we are dealing with 'a priori intuitions'; this automatically gives a content to our thought which is absent from the abstract employment of the categories. The conclusions of mathematics are arrived at both 'a priori and immediately' (A 732, B 760), whereas those of metaphysics must be derived by laborious argument.

Whether or not we accept Kant's explanation, it is a distinctive feature of his philosophy that he took mathematical truths to be synthetic a priori. At the same time he refused to countenance Plato's explanation of this synthetic a priori status, as deriving from the peculiar nature of mathematical objects: the abstract, immutable numbers and Forms. Kant also disagreed with Hume and Leibniz, both of whom had argued that mathematics is analytic. The question is, therefore, how can mathematics be synthetic a priori, and yet not provide knowledge of some mysterious and unobservable realm? In the *Inaugural Dissertation* Kant argued that the a priori nature of geometry derives from the subject, rather than from the object, of mathematical thought (I 70–2). It is this that led to his mature view that there can be a priori knowledge of space only if space enters into the nature of perception. Hence the theory of space as a 'form' of intuition.

Objective knowledge has, then, a double origin: sensibility and understanding. And just as the first must 'conform to' the second, so must the second 'conform to' the first; otherwise the transcendental synthesis of the two would be impossible. What does it mean to say that the understanding must 'conform to' the sensibility? Since time is the general form of all sensibility, the claim amounts to this: the categories must find their primary application in time, and be 'determined', or limited, accordingly. Thus the concept of substance must have, as its primary instance, not the monads of Leibniz, nor the abstract objects of the Platonic supersphere, but ordinary temporal things, which endure through time, and are subject to change. If such things are objective, then, by the theory that space is the form of outer sense, they must also be spatial. So to prove the 'objective validity' of the concept of substance is not to prove that the world consists of monads. The world consists rather of ordinary spatio-temporal objects. The philosophical proof of objectivity establishes the existence, not of an abstract, perspectiveless, world, but of the common-sense world of science and everyday perception: the very world which both Humean scepticism and Leibnizian metaphysics had thrown in doubt. It was therefore important to Kant to show, in his proof of objectivity, that the beliefs which he justified corresponded exactly to the laws which Newtonian science had laid down for all perceivable things.

The transcendental unity of apperception

The 'objective' deduction of the categories begins from the premise of self-consciousness, described, in characteristic language, as the 'transcendental unity of apperception'. It is important to understand this phrase which contains in embryo much of Kant's philosophy. 'Apperception' is a term taken from Leibnizian metaphysics; it refers to any experience of which the subject is able to say 'this is mine'. In other words, 'apperception' means 'self-conscious experience'. The unity of apperception consists in the '"I think" which can accompany all my perceptions' (B 131-2), to borrow again Kant's version of Descartes. It consists of my immediate awareness that simultaneous experiences belong to me. I know immediately that this thought, and this perception, are equally *mine*, in the sense of belonging to the unity of consciousness which defines my point of view. Doubt is here impossible: I could never be in the position that Dickens in *Hard Times* attributes to Mrs Gradgrind on her deathbed, knowing that there is a pain in the room somewhere, but not knowing that it is mine. This apprehension of unity is called 'transcendental' because I could never derive it from experience. I could not argue that, because this pain has such a quality, and this thought such another, they must belong to a single consciousness. If I did that, I could make a mistake; I could be in the absurd position of ascribing to myself some pain, thought or perception which belonged, not to me, but to some other consciousness. So the unity that I apprehend in my point of view is not a conclusion from experience, but a presupposition of experience. Its basis 'transcends' anything that experience could establish. As Kant sometimes puts it, the unity of consciousness 'precedes' all the data of intuition (A 107).

The transcendental unity of apperception provides the minimal description of our point of view. I can know at least one thing: that there is a unity of consciousness. To doubt this is to cease to be self-conscious, and so to cease to find significance in doubt. The task is to show that this point of view is possible only in an objective world.

The transcendental deduction

The objective deduction has the same 'transcendental' character as its premise. It is concerned to show that the truth of its conclusion is not a deduction from experience but presupposed in the *existence* of experience. The transcendental unity of apperception is possible only if the subject inhabits the kind of world which the categories describe: an objective world, in which things may be other than they seem. To put the argument in a nutshell: the unity of apperception describes the condition of subjectivity, in which everything is as it seems and seems as it is. But no one can have the point of view of subjectivity who does not have knowledge of objective truths. He must therefore belong to a world of things which can be other than they seem, and which exist independently of his own perspective.

An argument to that effect is hard to find, and it is significant that Kant was so dissatisfied with 'The Transcendental Deduction' that he rewrote it entirely for the second edition of the *Critique*, changing its emphasis from the subjective conclusion given above towards the objective deduction presently under discussion. Even so, the result is very obscure, and a further passage – 'The Refutation of Idealism' – was added in order to make the emphasis on objectivity more persuasive. The point of this 'refutation' was to show 'that we have experience, and not merely *imagination*, of outer things' by demonstrating that 'even our inner experience [*Erfahrung*], which for Descartes is indubitable, is possible only on the assumption of outer experience [i.e. experience of an objective world]' (B 275). The flavour of the argument is more apparent than its substance. At least the following three thoughts seem to be involved in it:

(i) Identifying experience. It is a common empiricist assumption that I can know my experience simply by observing it. But this is not so. I do not observe my experience, but only its object. Any knowledge of experience must therefore involve knowledge of its object. But I can have knowledge of the object only if I identify it as continuous. Nothing can have temporal

continuity without also having the capacity to exist when un-
observed. Its existence is therefore independent of my perception.

(ii) Identity through time. I can identify experience as mine
only if I locate it in time. I must therefore ascribe it to a subject
who exists in time and endures through time. My unity requires
my continuity. But to endure is to be substantial, and nothing
can be substantial unless it also enters into causal relations. I
endure only if my past explains my future. Otherwise there is
no difference between genuine duration and an infinite sequence of momentary selves. If I can be conscious of my experience at all, I can therefore conclude that I belong to a world to
which such categories as substance and cause are correctly applied, since they are correctly applied to me. A condition of
self-consciousness is, therefore, the existence of just that objective order which my experience suggests to me.

(iii) Ordering in time. I have privileged knowledge of *present*
experience. To know my experience is therefore to know it *as*
present. This is possible only if I distinguish in experience between *now* and *then*. Hence there is a 'temporal order' inherent
in perception, and I must know this order if I am to know
myself. But I can know it only if I can make reference to independent objects, and the regularities which govern them. Only
then will I be able to describe time as a dimension *in* which
experience occurs, rather than as a series of unrelated instants.
The reality of time is presupposed in experience. And the reality of time presupposes the reality of an objective sequence. It is
only by reference to that sequence, and to the enduring objects
that structure it, that I can identify my own perception.

None of those thoughts is clearer in the original than in my
brief résumé. It is fair to say that the transcendental deduction
has never been considered to provide a satisfactory argument.
In all its versions it involves a transition from the *unity* of consciousness to the *identity* of the subject through time. Hume
pointed out that the slide from unity to identity is involved in
all our claims to objective knowledge; he also thought that it
could never be justified. Kant did not find the terms with which

to answer Hume. Nevertheless his enterprise has appealed to many subsequent philosophers, and the transcendental deduction has been revived in recent years, most notably by Ludwig Wittgenstein (1889–1951). In the famous 'private language' argument in his *Philosophical Investigations* Wittgenstein argues that there can be no knowledge of experience which does not presuppose reference to a public world. I can know my own experience immediately and incorrigibly, but only because I apply to it concepts which gain their sense from public usage. And public usage describes a reality observable to others besides myself. The publicity of my language guarantees the objectivity of its reference. Wittgenstein's argument – which has seemed persuasive to many – shares the premise and the conclusion of the transcendental deduction. It relies, however, not on metaphysical doctrines about time, but on doctrines about reference and meaning.

If valid, the transcendental deduction achieves a result of immense significance. It establishes the objectivity of my world while assuming no more than my point of view on it. Descartes, in the proof of the external world offered in his *Meditations*, tried to step outside the point of view of the subject by establishing the existence of an omniscient God: the world is then validated as an object of God's (perspectiveless) awareness. The essence of Kant's 'transcendental' method lies in its egocentricity. All the questions that I can ask I must ask from the standpoint that is mine; therefore they must bear the marks of my perspective, which is the perspective of 'possible experience'. The answer to them is not to be found in the attempt to rise to the standpoint of the reasoning being who knows without experience, but to find, within my experience itself, the response to sceptical enquiry. The transcendental method finds the answer to every philosophical question in the presuppositions of the perspective from which it must be asked.

Principles

Kant argues that every category corresponds to a principle, whose truth is presupposed in its application. Principles are 'rules for the objective employment' of the categories (A 161, B 200). These principles are a priori truths, and they have two aspects. They say how we must think if we are to think at all; and, in their objective aspect, they say how the world must be if it is to be intelligible. Through these principles, the categories 'prescribe laws a priori to appearances, and therefore to nature' (B 163). That is to say, they lay down synthetic a priori truths concerning the world of everyday and scientific observation. They are not a priori truths about 'things-in-themselves'. They do not give knowledge of a world described without reference to our perception. Synthetic a priori knowledge is only of 'things which may be the objects of possible experience' (B 148). In this area, the principles state objective and necessary truths, since the categories 'relate of necessity and a priori to the objects of experience, for the reason that only by means of them can any object of experience be thought' (A 110). The limitation to the 'objects of possible experience' is vital to Kant's philosophy, and he repeatedly emphasises that 'outside the field of possible experience there can be no synthetic a priori principles' (A 248, B 305). We must always bear in mind that Kant wishes to admit a priori knowledge, but also to deny the possibility of the perspectiveless metaphysics of Leibniz.

I have chosen to concentrate on the categories of substance and cause. Kant associated these with a third, that of community, or reciprocal interaction. These concepts had been the principal objects of Hume's sceptical attack. They were also crucial to Leibniz's metaphysics, substance being the idea from which Leibniz began, and the 'Principle of Sufficient Reason', associated by Kant with causality (A 200–1, B 246), being the principle which governed his argument. Kant's discussion of these concepts is of great and lasting interest. He placed them at the heart of the question of objectivity, and expressed, in their analysis, what he took to be the metaphysical foundations of physical science. He derives their associated principles in a section called 'Analogies of Experience', and it is here that Kant makes some of his most revolutionary suggestions concerning the nature of objective knowledge.

Kant's division of all philosophical thought into elements of four and three is obsessive. But there is a special reason, when talking of substance and causality, for his insistence that there should be a third basic concept associated with these; namely, that Kant wished his results to correspond to the three Newtonian laws of motion. Scientific explanation depends upon principles of method: being presupposed in scientific enquiry, these principles cannot be proved through it. Kant believed that such principles would be reflected in basic scientific laws; and it is one of the tasks of metaphysics to provide grounds for their acceptance.

The physical science of Kant's day seemed to assume a priori the existence of universal causation, and of reciprocal interaction. It assumed that it must explain, not the *existence* of matter, but the changes undergone by it. It assumed the need for a law of conservation, according to which, in all changes, some fundamental quantity remains unaltered. It is just such assumptions, Kant thought, that had guided Newton in the formulation of his laws of motion. Kant therefore attempts, in deriving his principles, to establish the 'validity of universal laws of nature as laws of the understanding' (M 74), arguing further that all the fundamental laws of the new astronomy can be seen, on reflection, to rest on principles that are valid a priori (M 83).

The attempt to uphold the Newtonian mechanics is mixed with an attack on Hume's scepticism about causality. Kant tries to show that causal relations are necessary, both in the sense that it is necessary that objects enter into them (there is no event without a cause), and also in the sense that they are themselves a species of necessary connection.

The 'Analogies' contain too many arguments to be treated in detail here. Like other crucial passages of the Analytic, they were substantially rewritten for the second edition, the actual statement of the 'principles' undergoing significant revisions. But two theses deserve singling out on account of their subsequent importance. First, Kant argues that all explanation of change requires the postulation of an unchanging substance, and uses this as proof of the validity of a fundamental 'law of conservation' in science. His arguments provide one of the most important insights into the nature of scientific method since Descartes, and a clear move in the direction of the modern doctrine of the 'unity of science'. According to one version of this doctrine, there is a single law of conservation involved in the explanation of every change, and hence a single stuff (for example, energy), whose laws of transformation govern the whole of nature.

Secondly, Kant defends, in the second Analogy, the important metaphysical doctrine that 'the relation of cause to effect is the condition of the objective validity of our empirical judgements' (A 202, B 247). It is only because we can find causal connections in our world that we can postulate its objectivity. This is a consequence of the connection between objectivity and duration: it is because things endure that I can distinguish their appearance from their reality. But they can endure only if there is a thread of causal connection which unites their temporal parts. This table is as it is *because* it was as it was. The dependence of objectivity on causality is matched by a similar dependence of causality on substance: it is only on the assumption of enduring things that our causal laws gain application. 'Causality leads to the concept of action, this in turn to the concept of force, and thereby to the concept of substance' (A 204). We could put the point briefly by saying that we discover how things really are only by finding causes for how they seem, and we find causes only by postulating a realm of enduring things.

So the thought of an independent object involves thoughts about causality, and causality, Kant argues, is a species of necessity. To know any truth about the world is therefore to have knowledge of necessities: of what must be and of what might have been. This thesis radically contradicts the empiricist view that there are no necessities in nature, and also those modern theories which believe that our basic thoughts about the actual involve mental operations that are simpler than those involved in grasping the necessary and the possible.

All these striking theses emerge from an attempt to give what one might call a fully 'enriched' account of the objectivity of the physical world. Any philosopher who takes Kant's arguments seriously will see how difficult it is to 'reduce' the idea of an objective world to a mere synopsis of experience. Hence he will recognise the implausibility, not only of the scepticism which Kant attacked, but also of the empiricist theory of knowledge from which it began.

Conclusion

The principles are valid a priori, but only in the case of the 'objects of possible experience'. The empiricists were wrong in rejecting the possibility of such a priori principles, but right in their assumption that our own perspective on the world is in some measure a constituent of our knowledge. We can know the world a priori only in so far as it is possible for it to present an appearance to our point of view. It is vain to attempt to rise above that point of view and know the world 'as it is in itself', independently of any possible perception. Thus all attempts to prove Leibniz's Principle of Sufficient Reason 'have, by the universal admission of those concerned, been fruitless' (A 783, B 811). But the 'transcendental' equivalent of the principle, Kant argues, is provable: the principle of sufficient reason then becomes the law of causality, the law that every event in the empirical world is bound by causal connections. This is an a priori truth, but only of the 'world of appearance', and therefore only of events in time. Despite Kant's swaggering self-confidence in this matter, many Leibnizians felt that they *had* offered a proof of the Principle of Sufficient Reason – Baumgarten, for one. And one of Baumgarten's disciples, Eberhard, attempted to show that the critical philosophy was no more than a restatement of the Leibnizian system, the Principle of Sufficient Reason being both necessary to Kant's enterprise and provable a priori. This was one of the few criticisms of the *Critique* to which Kant felt obliged to reply (in *On a Discovery*, published in 1790). Kant demonstrates the impossibility of proving the Principle 'without relation to sensible intuition' (K 113), and emphasises the helplessness of pure reason to advance beyond concepts to any substantial truth about the world. The

Principle of Sufficient Reason can be established, he argues, only by his 'transcendental' method, which relates the objects of knowledge to the capacities of the knower, and proves a priori only those laws which determine the conditions of experience.

The vain attempt of the Leibnizians to found knowledge in 'pure reason' alone is the topic of the Dialectic. In following the outline of Kant's criticisms we shall be able to see exactly what he meant by 'transcendental idealism', and why he thought it could provide the middle course between empiricism and rationalism.

4 The logic of illusion

While the understanding, properly employed, yields genuine, objective, knowledge, it also contains a temptation to illusion. It is this temptation that Kant attempts to diagnose and criticise in his examination of 'pure reason', and once again his argument has a subjective and an objective side. He describes a particular faculty, reason, in its illegitimate employment; he also demolishes all the claims to knowledge which that faculty tempts us to make. His subject-matter in the Dialectic is rationalist metaphysics, and he divides metaphysics into three parts – rational psychology, concerning the nature of the soul, cosmology, concerning the nature of the universe and our status within it, and theology, concerning the existence of God. He then goes on to argue that each proceeds in accordance with its own kind of illusory argument, not towards truth, but towards fallacy. The diagnosis of these errors follows a common pattern. Each attempt by pure reason to establish the metaphysical doctrines towards which it is impelled transgresses the limits of experience, applying concepts in a manner that is 'unconditioned' by the faculty of intuition. Since it is only through the synthesis of concept and intuition that judgement is formed, this attempt cannot produce knowledge. On the contrary, concepts, divorced from their 'empirical conditions', are empty. 'The pure concepts of the understanding can *never* admit of *transcendental* but *always* only of *empirical* employment' (A 246, B 303). At the same time, since concepts contain within themselves this tendency towards 'unconditioned' application, it is an inevitable disease of the understanding that 'pure reason' should usurp its functions, and the categories be transformed from instruments of knowledge into those instruments of illusion which Kant calls 'ideas'.

Here we need to take another look at transcendental idealism, in order to see exactly what it is that Kant regards himself as having established in the Analytic. We find a crucial ambiguity in Kant's doctrines, which persists through the second and third *Critiques*.

Appearance and reality

Kant often describes transcendental idealism as the doctrine that we have a priori knowledge only of 'appearances' and not of 'things as they are in themselves' (or 'things-in-themselves'). His followers and critics disputed heatedly over the 'thing-in-itself'. Moses Mendelssohn thought of it as a distinct entity, so that an appearance is one thing, the thing-in-itself another. Others, under the influence of Kant's pupil J. S. Beck, took the phrase 'thing-in-itself' to refer to a way of describing the very same object which we also know as an appearance. Kant lends support to this second interpretation in his correspondence with Beck, in many passages of the *Critique of Practical Reason*, and in a letter to one of its principal advocates: 'All objects that can be given to us can be conceptualised in two ways: on the one hand, as appearances; on the other hand, as things in themselves' (C 103n.). But there is no doubt that his mind was not made up about the matter, and this led to a crucial ambiguity in the critical philosophy.

Kant also says that the categories can be applied to 'phenomena', but not to 'noumena'. A phenomenon is an 'object of possible experience', whereas a noumenon is an object knowable to thought alone, and which it does not make sense to describe as the object of experience. It is natural to connect the two distinctions, and to assume that Kant believes appearances, or phenomena, to be knowable through experience, and 'things-in-themselves' to be mere noumena, not knowable at all since nothing is knowable in thought alone. Kant says, for example, that the concept of a 'noumenon' can be used only negatively, to designate the limit of our knowledge, and not positively, to designate things as they are in themselves. So that 'The division of objects into phenomena and noumena, and the world into a world of the senses and a world of the under-standing, is . . . quite inadmissible in the positive sense' (A 255,

B 311). In which case, the 'thing-in-itself' is not an entity, but a term standing proxy for the unrealisable ideal of perspectiveless knowledge.

The ambiguity in Kant's account is illustrated by the term 'appearance', which is taken sometimes in a transitive, sometimes in an intransitive, sense. Kant sometimes writes as though appearances are 'appearances of' something, whose reality is hidden from us. At other times, he writes as though appearances were independent entities, which derive their name from the fact that we observe and discover their nature. In this second sense, the word 'appearance' corresponds to our idea of a physical object. An appearance can be observed; it is situated in space; it enters into causal relations with other appearances and with the being who observes them. It is governed by scientific laws, and is or can be an object of discovery. It may be as it seems, and also other than it seems. It can have both secondary qualities (qualities which an object possesses only in relation to a particular sensory experience) and primary qualities (qualities which belong to its inner constitution) (A 28–9). In short, appearances possess all the characteristics of physical objects. To say that an appearance is also an appearance *of* something is surely incoherent. For, by Kant's own theory, the 'something' which supposedly underlies appearance could only be a 'noumenon', and about noumena nothing significant can be said. In particular, it makes no sense (or, at least, is devoid of content) to say that a noumenon causes, or stands in any other relation to, an appearance. (Kant's critics – such as Mendelssohn and G. E. Schulze – were quick to seize on this point, and put it forward as the principal weakness of the transcendental philosophy.) Sometimes indeed Kant writes as though every object is an appearance *of* some 'thing-in-itself'. But since this is inconsistent with his theory of knowledge (which allows him neither to know nor even to mean what he purports to say) we must, for the moment, consider the thing-in-itself to be a nonentity. As we shall see, there are countervailing reasons which caused Kant to deny his own official theory. But it is impossible to proceed if we allow these reasons, and the rival doctrines which stem from them, to gain precedence at this juncture.

Phenomena and noumena

The first edition of the *Critique* contained a lengthy exposition of the theory of transcendental idealism. This was deleted by Kant from the second edition, perhaps because it gave too much encouragement to the ambiguity described above. Kant also added the section called 'The Refutation of Idealism' (see above, pp. 33–5), which purports to provide a positive proof of objectivity, and a disproof of the 'empirical idealism' attributed to Berkeley. Empirical idealism is the view that 'empirical' objects are nothing but perceptions, and that the world of science has no reality beyond the experience of the observer. All empirical objects become 'ideal' entities, with no reality outside our conception of them. By contrast, Kant argues, transcendental idealism is a form of empirical realism: it implies that empirical objects are real.

Kant's assertion that transcendental idealism entails empirical realism is difficult to interpret. He argues, for example, that space and time are empirically real and *also* transcendentally ideal (A 28, B 44). This could mean that, if we take an empirical perspective, so to speak, then we acknowledge the reality of space and time; while, from the transcendental point of view, these things are 'nothing at all' (ibid.). However, the idea of a transcendental point of view is, as Kant recognises, highly contentious. It is not a point of view that is available to us, and therefore not something of which we can have a positive conception. A simpler reading of Kant's theory is the following: empirical objects are real, whereas transcendental objects are ideal. A transcendental object is not perceivable, and does not belong to the world of space, time and causality. The 'monad' of Leibniz is such an object, and must therefore always remain a mere idea in the mind that conceives it, with no independent reality. But what are empirical objects? The answer that suggests itself is 'whatever objects are discovered or postulated through experience'.

The above states a metaphysical view which exactly corresponds to Kant's theory of knowledge. In the last analysis, it does not matter whether we describe the distinction between the empirical and the transcendental object as a distinction between that which exists and that which does not, or as a distinction between that which is knowable and that which is not. For, to borrow a remark of Wittgenstein's, 'a nothing would do as well as a something about which nothing can be said'. It seems then that the distinction corresponds again to that between phenomena and noumena, the first being knowable, the second unknowable, since the concept of a noumenon can be employed only negatively, in order to mark out the limits of experience. All noumena are transcendental objects, and all transcendental objects, being merely 'intelligible' (i.e. not knowable through experience), are noumena. So it would seem that the three distinctions coincide: phenomenon/noumenon; empirical object/ transcendental object; appearance/thing-in-itself. In a lengthy discussion of Leibniz which forms the bridging passage between the Analytic and the Dialectic this is, in effect, what Kant says (especially A 288–9, B 344–6). Many scholars do not accept this interpretation; but it seems to me that, if we do not accept it, we attribute to Kant more inconsistency than his dexterity can sustain.

It is not surprising, therefore, to find that the ambiguity which surrounds Kant's doctrine of 'appearance' attaches also to his concept of the 'phenomenon'. This term is interpreted, sometimes as denoting a real perceivable object which exists independently of the observer, sometimes as denoting a mental 'representation' (or, in modern parlance, 'intentional object'). Under the latter interpretation the phenomenon becomes subjective (it is as it seems, and seems as it is). To establish its existence is to provide no guarantee of objectivity. No significant distinction would then remain between Kant's position (that we can have knowledge of phenomena) and the empirical idealism which he claims to reject. Even Leibniz admitted more objectivity into our 'point of view' than the empirical idealist, since he introduced the notion of the 'well-founded phenomenon' (see above, pp. 15–16), according to which the stability of appearances is sufficient to warrant the distinction between being and seeming. Leibniz's approach to the 'phenomenal world' certainly influenced Kant, more perhaps than he cared to admit. But he wanted to go further in the direction of establishing the objectivity of the world of appearance, not less far.

It is clear from all this that the only acceptable interpretation of the terms 'phenomenon', 'appearance', and 'empirical object' is as denoting items in the physical world. Appearances include tables, chairs, and other such visible things; they also include entities that are observable only through their effects, such as atoms (A 442, B 470) and the most distant stars (A 496, B 524). These 'theoretical' entities also have the reality which comes from existence in space and time, and from the order imposed by the categories. They too are perceivable, in the sense of entering into specific causal relations with the mind which knows them. In other words, any object of scientific investigation is a 'phenomenon', and all phenomena are knowable in principle. But nothing else is knowable. 'Nothing is really given us save perception and the empirical advance [i.e. scientific inference] from this to other possible perceptions' (A 493, B 521). As for the idea of a noumenon, this is 'not the concept of an object' but a 'problem unavoidably bound up with the limitation of our sensibility' (A 287, B 344).

The unconditioned

Kant's intention in the Dialectic is to show that we cannot know the 'world as it is', meaning the world conceived apart from the perspective of the knower. We must not, as Kant puts it, aspire to 'unconditioned' knowledge. At the same time, it seems inevitable that we should do so. Every time we establish something by argument, we assume the truth of the premise. The premise therefore describes the 'condition' under which the conclusion is true. But what about the truth of this condition? That too must be established by argument, and will turn out to possess its truth only 'conditionally'. Hence reason (in its guise

as inference) inevitably leads us to search for the 'unconditioned', the ultimate premise whose truth is derived from no
other source. This 'idea' of reason contains the source of all
metaphysical illusion. For all knowledge that we can legitimately claim is subject to the 'conditions' of possible experience. To
aspire to knowledge of the unconditioned is to aspire beyond
the conditions which make knowledge possible.

The effort of transcendence is, Kant argues, inevitable. Not
only do we seek to transcend the conditions contained in the
possibility of experience. We also seek to know the world 'as it
is', free from the conditions to which it may be subject by such
categories as substance and cause. These enterprises are in fact
one and the same; for, as the Analytic shows, the two sets of
conditions are identical. In each case the advance of reason towards the 'unconditioned' is the pursuit of knowledge untainted
by perspective. Reason always aims to view the world, as Leibniz had viewed it, from no point of view. ✳

'Pure reason'

From the standpoint of Kant's theory of knowledge, reason
must be seen as the highest of cognitive faculties, under which
all that is distinctive of self-knowledge is subsumed. Apart from
its use in understanding (forming judgements), reason can be
employed legitimately in two further ways: practically, and in
carrying out inferences. Practical reason cannot be regarded as a
branch of the understanding since it does not issue in judgements (it makes no claims about the true and the false). Nevertheless its use is legitimate: I can reason what to do, and my
action can be a legitimate outcome of this process. Inference,
which is the practice of deriving the logical consequences of a
judgement, is also legitimate. But, unlike understanding, it em-
ploys no concepts of its own (for an inference which, as it were,
'adds a concept' to the premise is for that reason invalid).

✳ It is only when *pure* reason enters our thoughts that the 'logic
of illusion' begins to beguile us. Pure reason is distinguished by
the fact that it tries to make judgements of its own, using, not
concepts, but 'ideas' from which all empirical conditions have

been removed. The logic of illusion is 'dialectical': it must inevitably end in fallacy and contradiction. This tendency towards fallacy is not accidental, but intrinsic. There is no way in which reason can set out to know the world through 'ideas' and avoid the errors that lie in wait for it. These errors have already been committed, just as soon as we leave the knowable realms of experience and embark on the journey towards the 'unconditioned' world beyond. At the same time there is no way in which we can avoid the temptation towards this vain journey into the transcendental. Our very possession of a point of view on the world creates the 'idea' of a world seen from no point of view. Thus we strive always 'to find for the conditioned knowledge of the understanding, the unconditioned, whereby its unity might be brought to completion' (A 307, B 364).

Pure reason and metaphysics

I have already drawn attention to Kant's important threefold division of the subject-matter of speculative metaphysics. In 'transcendental psychology' reason generates its doctrines of the soul; in rational cosmology it attempts to describe the world in its 'unconditioned totality'; in theology, it creates the idea of the perfect being who presides over a transcendent world. By a contrivance, Kant reconciles this division with the traditional view, that 'metaphysics has as the proper object of its enquiries three ideas only: *God*, *freedom* and *immortality*' (B 395n.). The idea of freedom is assigned to cosmology, on the grounds that all the metaphysical problems created by this idea stem from the belief that there is something – the moral agent – which is both in the world of nature and also outside it. This is one of the most important of Kant's doctrines. But I shall postpone discussion of it until the chapter which follows.

Cosmology

The illusions of cosmology are called 'antinomies'. An 'antinomy' is the peculiar fallacy which enables us to derive both a proposition and its negation from the same premise. According to Kant antinomies are not genuine contradictions, since both of the propositions which constitute them are false, being based on a false assumption. He entitles this 'kind of opposition *dialectical*, and that of contradictories *analytical*' (A 504, B 532). He offers various tortuous explanations of how a proposition and its negation can both be false, and it is perhaps unnecessary to be detained by this puzzling piece of logic. Kant's point is that, in deriving each side of an antinomy, the same false assumption must be made. The purpose of his 'critique' is to root out this false assumption and show it to stem from the application of one of reason's 'ideas'. The assumption involved in cosmology is that we can think of the world in its 'unconditioned totality'. This would be possible only by transcending the perspective of 'possible experience' and trying to see all nature as a whole, from a perspective outside of it. The illusory nature of this idea is displayed by the fact that, from the premise of such a transcendent perspective, a 'dialectical' contradiction follows.

Suppose, for example, that I allow myself to entertain the idea of the whole world of nature, as it is situated in space and time. If I now attempt to apply the idea in judgement, I must pass beyond my empirical vision in order to grasp the totality of all objects of experience. I must attempt to envisage the whole of nature, independently of my particular perspective within it. If I could do that, I could ask myself: Is this totality limited or unlimited in space and time? Does it, or does it not, have boundaries? I find myself equally able to prove both conclusions. I can prove, for example, that the world must have a beginning in time (otherwise an infinite sequence of events must have already elapsed, and, Kant argues, a 'completed infinity' is an absurd idea). I can equally prove that it must have no beginning in time (for if it had a beginning, then there must be a reason why it began when it did, which is to suppose, absurdly, that a particular time has a causal property, or a capacity to 'bring into being', independently of the events which occupy it).

A similar contradiction can be derived from the assumption that the world as a whole has an explanation for its existence.

From that assumption, I can prove that the world is causally self-dependent, consisting of an infinite chain of causes linking each moment to its predecessor. For the idea of a beginning to this series – the idea of a 'first cause' – is absurd, leading automatically to the question 'What caused the beginning?', to which there is no coherent answer. I can equally prove that the world is causally dependent, deriving its existence from some being which is 'cause of itself', or *causa sui*. For if there were no such being, then none of the causes in the sequence of nature would explain the existence of its effect. In which case, nothing in nature would have an explanation, and it would be impossible to say why anything should exist at all.

Such antinomies result from the attempt to reach beyond the perspective of experience to the absolute vantage-point from which the totality of things (and hence the world 'as it is in itself') can be surveyed. If we suppose nature to be a thing-in-itself – i.e. if we remove from the concept of nature the reference to any possible experience through which it is observed – then the proofs of the antinomies are well-grounded. 'The conflict which results from the propositions thus obtained shows, however, that there is a fallacy in this assumption, and so leads us to the discovery of the true constitution of things, as objects of the senses' (A 507, B 537). The idea of 'absolute totality' holds only of 'things-in-themselves' (A 506, B 534), which is to say, of nothing knowable. For example, the concept of cause, which we can apply *within* the realm of empirical objects in order to designate their relations, becomes empty when lifted out of that realm and applied to the world as a whole. It is then applied beyond the empirical conditions which justify its application, and so leads inevitably to contradiction.

Nevertheless, Kant argues, these antinomies are not to be lightly dismissed as errors no sooner perceived than forgone. The assumption of totality which generates them is both the cause and the effect of all that is most serious in science. Suppose we were to accept the 'big bang' hypothesis concerning the origin of the universe. Only a short-sighted person would think that we have then answered the question how the world began.

For what caused the bang? Any answer will suppose that something already existed. So the hypothesis cannot explain the origin of things. The quest for an origin leads us forever backwards into the past. But either it is unsatisfiable – in which case, how does cosmology explain the *existence* of the world? – or it comes to rest in the postulation of a *causa sui* – in which case, we have left the scientific question unanswered and taken refuge in theology. Science itself pushes us towards the antinomy, by forcing us always to the limits of nature. But how can I know those limits if I cannot also transcend them?

Kant engages in an elaborate diagnosis of the antinomies, arguing that the two sides always correspond to rationalism and empiricism respectively, and he takes the opportunity to explore again the various errors of those philosophies. The resulting discussion is exceedingly complex, and has produced as much philosophical commentary as anything in the first *Critique*. Kant's love of system leads him to combine arguments of very different import and quality. But behind the profusion of reasoning lies one of the acutest discussions of scientific method to have issued from the pen of a philosopher. A reading of Kant's discussion inspired men as diverse as Hegel and Einstein, and few can fail to be puzzled by the problems that Kant unearths. How *can* I view the world in its totality? And yet, how can there be explanation if I cannot? How can I explain the existence of anything, if I cannot explain the existence of everything? If I am confined for ever within my own point of view, how can I penetrate the mystery of nature?

Theology

I have discussed the first and fourth of Kant's antinomies. The latter brings us to theology, and to Kant's subsequent suggestion that the idea of a *causa sui* is itself empty, and can be applied in judgement only so as to generate a contradiction. In the chapter entitled 'The Ideal of Reason', Kant reviews the traditional arguments for the existence of God, and imposes upon them a now famous classification. There are, he says, only three kinds of argument for God's existence, the 'cosmological', the 'ontological' and the 'physico-theological'. The first kind comprises all arguments which, proceding from some contingent fact about the world, and from the question '*Why* is it so?', postulate the existence of a necessary being. A version of this is the 'first cause' argument discussed above: only if the series of causes begins in a *causa sui* can any contingent fact be finally explained. Of the second kind are all arguments which, in order to free themselves from contingent premises (which, because they might be false, might also be doubted), attempt to prove the existence of God from the concept of God. Of the third kind are all arguments from 'design', which begin from the premise of some good in nature, and argue by analogy to the perfection of its cause.

Kant says of the argument from design that it 'always deserves to be mentioned with respect. It is the oldest, the clearest, and the most consonant with human reason. It enlivens the study of nature, just as it itself derives its existence and gains ever new strength from that source' (A 623, B 651). In the third *Critique* he explains in more detail why this argument appealed to him. Kant was no atheist, and was perturbed by Hume's posthumous *Dialogues on Natural Religion*, the German version of which appeared as the *Critique* was being prepared for the press. There was time for Kant to wonder about Hume's motives, but not to consider his arguments (A 745, B 773). Hume foreshadows Kant's own critique of rational theology. But he is particularly dismissive of the argument from design, arguing that it proves either nothing at all (since there is no genuine analogy between the perfections of nature and the perfections of art) or , at best, the existence of a being no more perfect than the world of his creation. Kant too was unsatisfied by the argument from design. But although he thought of it as invalid, at the same time he felt it to be the expression of a true presentiment. Hence he tried to provide a wholly novel elucidation of it, from the point of view not of the first but of the third *Critique*.

Considered as an intellectual proof, the argument from design can never be more cogent than the cosmological proof, upon which it depends (A 630, B 658). For it is only on the assumption of ultimate explanation that the argument from design can operate. That assumption carries no weight unless the cosmological proof is valid. We must show that we can step outside nature, in order to postulate the existence of a transcendent, necessary being. But what entitles us to postulate such a being? According to Kant, only the ontological argument will answer that question. For if we ask ourselves how something can be cause of itself, or how it can exist by necessity, the answer must be found in the concept of that thing. The concept of the divine being must explain his existence. This can be true only if the existence of God *follows* from the concept of God, since it is only by logical relations that a concept can explain anything. So, in the end, all three arguments reduce to this single one.

In its traditional forms the ontological argument proves not only the existence, but also the perfection of God. Neither of the other arguments seems able to prove God's absolute perfection: once again, they must rely on the ontological argument to give intellectual grounds for religious sentiment. The ontological argument proceeds as follows. God is an all-perfect being. Among perfections we must count moral goodness, power and freedom. But we must also count existence. For the concept of an existent x is the concept of something more perfect than an x; to take away existence is to take away perfection. So existence is a perfection. Hence it follows from the idea of God, as an all-perfect being, that God exists.

Kant's rebuttal of this argument is famous for its anticipation of a doctrine of modern logic – the doctrine that existence is not a predicate. (When I say that John exists, is bald, and eats oysters, I attribute to John not three properties, but two.) Leibniz, in his discussion of contingency, had already recognised that existence is quite different from ordinary predicates. Nevertheless, he accepted the ontological argument, and did not see the logical consequence of his philosophy. To say that an x exists is to add nothing to its concept: it is to say that the concept has an instance. Indeed, there is already a fallacy (Kant even says a contradiction) involved in introducing existence into the concept of a thing (A 597, B 625). For it then becomes empty to assert that the thing exists. The assertion makes no advance from concept to reality. And so it affirms the existence of nothing. The ontological argument says that existence is a perfection. But it cannot be a perfection, since it is not a property. If the argument were valid, Kant thinks, it would follow that the judgement that God exists expresses an analytic truth. The theory that existence is not a predicate implies, however, that all existential propositions are synthetic (A 598, B 626).

The regulative employment of the ideas of reason

Having completed his denunciation of the 'logic of illusion' Kant goes on to argue, at considerable length, and in a relaxed, expansive style appropriate to a writer whose intellectual labour is ended, that there is, after all, a legitimate use for the ideas of reason. Such ideas as that of unconditioned totality, and of the perfect creator who exists of necessity, generate illusions when considered in their 'constitutive' role: that is, when considered as descriptions of reality. The correct way to see them, however, is as 'regulative principles' (A 644, B 672). If we act as if these ideas were true of reality, then we are led to formulate true hypotheses. The ideas of order and totality, for example, lead us to propose ever wider and simpler laws, in terms of which the empirical world becomes ever more intelligible. This 'regulative' employment of the ideas is an employment from within the standpoint of experience. The constitutive employment attempts to transcend that standpoint, into the illusory realm of reason. The contradictions do not stem from the ideas themselves (which are not contradictory but merely empty); they stem from their wrong application.

Thus 'the ideal of a supreme being is nothing but a *regulative principle* of reason, which directs us to look upon all connection in the world as if it originated from an all-sufficient and necessary cause' (A 619, B 647). Considered thus it is the source, not of illusion, but of knowledge. The knowledge that it leads to remains circumscribed by the conditions of possible experience: in other words it conforms to the categories, and does not reach beyond their legitimate territory into a transcendent realm. The idea 'does not show us how an object is constituted, but how, under its guidance, we should *seek* to determine the constitution and connection of the objects of experience' (A 671, B 699). Thus reason is led back from its vain speculations to the empirical world, trading the illusions of metaphysics for the realities of empirical science.

The soul

Kant's discussion of the soul, and of the concept of the 'self' from which it gains its initial description, is among the most subtle parts of his philosophy. The account is given in two complex arguments: the first at the beginning of the Dialectic, in which he attacks the rationalist doctrines of the soul; the second in the third antinomy, and in the *Critique of Practical Reason*, in which he describes the nature of morality.

The 'Paralogisms of Pure Reason', which deal with the rationalist doctrines of the soul, were substantially revised for the second edition, perhaps because this aspect of the critical philosophy forms part of the multi-faceted argument of the transcendental deduction, with which Kant had remained so dissatisfied. Kant's argument in the Analytic had begun by recognising the peculiar reality of self-consciousness. I have a privileged awareness of my states of mind, and this is an 'original' or 'transcendental' act of understanding. The rationalists had sought to deduce from this privileged knowledge a specific theory of its object. They had thought that, because of the immediacy of self-awareness, the self must be a genuine object of consciousness. In the act of self-awareness I am presented with the 'I' which is aware. I can maintain this self-awareness even while doubting every other thing. Moreover, I am necessarily aware of my unity. Finally, I have an intuitive sense of my continuity through time: this cannot be derived from the observation of my body, or from any other external source. It therefore seems natural to conclude that I know myself to be substantial, indivisible, enduring, perhaps even immortal, on the basis of the fact of self-awareness alone. Such, Kant thought, was

Descartes' argument. Nor is the conclusion an eccentricity of the 'Cartesian' view of consciousness. Like all the illusions of reason, it is one into which we are tempted just as soon as we begin to reflect on the datum before us. Every rational being must be tempted to think that the peculiar immediacy and inviolability of self-awareness guarantees its content. In the midst of every doubt, I may yet know this thing which is me, and, reason assures me, this intimate acquaintance with my own nature gives grounds for the belief in the immateriality of the soul.

The reasoning is erroneous, since it moves from the purely *formal* unity of apperception to the substantial unity affirmed in the doctrine of the soul. 'The unity of consciousness which underlies the categories is . . . mistaken for an intuition of the subject as object, and the category of substance is then applied to it' (B 421). Although the transcendental unity of apperception assures me that there is a unity in my present consciousness, it tells me nothing else about the kind of thing which bears it. It does not tell me that I am a substance (i.e. an independently existing object) as opposed to an 'accident' or property. (For example it does not refute the view that the mind is a complex property of the body.) It is 'quite impossible, by means of . . . simple self-consciousness to determine the manner in which I exist, whether it be as substance or accident' (B 420). If I cannot deduce that I am a substance, so much the less can I deduce that I am indivisible, indestructible or immortal. The unity of consciousness does not even assure me that there is something in the empirical world to which the term 'I' applies. For the peculiar features of self-consciousness summarised under the idea of a transcendental unity of apperception are simply features of a 'point of view' on the world. The 'I' as thereby described is not part of the world but a perspective upon it (a way things seem). 'For the I is not a concept but only a designation of the object of inner sense in so far as we know it through no further predicate' (M 98). To study the peculiarities of our self-awareness is, then, to study no item *in* the world. It is rather to explore that limiting point of empirical knowledge. 'The subject of the categories cannot by thinking the categories acquire a concept of itself as an object of the categories' (B 422). It is no more possible for me to make the 'I' into the object of consciousness than it is to observe the limits of my own visual field. 'I' is the expression of my perspective, but denotes no item within it.

The conclusion that Kant draws is this. There is a gap between the premise of 'transcendental psychology' – the transcendental unity of apperception – and its conclusion – the substantiality of the soul. Because the first describes a point of view on the world, and the second an item in the world, it is impossible that reason should take us validly from the one to the other. Whether correct or not, Kant's suggestion has provided the corner-stone of many subsequent philosophies of the self, from that of Schopenhauer to those of Husserl, Heidegger and Wittgenstein.

Sometimes Kant implies that the 'I' of self awareness refers to a transcendental object. For it might seem that, having proved that the 'I' is not part of the empirical world, Kant has given us reason to refer it to the world of the thing-in-itself which lies beyond experience. This is not a legitimate conclusion from his argument, but, on the contrary, another, more subtle reiteration of the fallacy that it was designed to expose. Nevertheless it is a conclusion which Kant was inclined to countenance, since, without it, he thought morality would not be possible. Kant sought for a positive doctrine of the soul, not through pure reason, but through practical reason (B 430–1). In order to understand this doctrine we must therefore explore his description of the moral life of the rational agent.

5 The categorical imperative

Kant's *Critique of Practical Reason* was preceded by a brilliant résumé of his moral viewpoint, the *Foundations of the Metaphysic of Morals*. These works treat of 'practical reason: in using this expression Kant was consciously reviving the ancient contrast between theoretical and practical knowledge. All rational beings recognise the distinction between knowing the truth and knowing what to do about it. Judgements and decisions may each be based on, and amended through, reason, but only the first can be true or false. Hence there must be an employment of our rational faculties which does not have truth, but something else, as its aim. What is this something else? Aristotle said happiness; Kant says duty. It is in the analysis of the idea of duty that Kant's distinctive moral vision is expressed.

Suppose we establish the objectivity of judgement, and provide the necessary metaphysical grounding to those scientific principles which underlie the process of discovery. There remains another problem of objectivity, raised by practical, rather than theoretical, knowledge. Can we know what to do objectively, or must we simply rely on our subjective inclination to guide us? It is to this problem that Kant addressed himself, producing the most metaphysical and abstract basis that has ever been given for the common intuitions of morality.

The antinomy of freedom

The starting-point of Kant's ethics is the concept of freedom. According to his famous maxim that 'ought implies can', the right action must always be possible: which is to say, I must always be free to perform it. The moral agent 'judges that he can do a certain thing because he is conscious that he ought, and he recognises that he is free, a fact which, but for the moral law, he would never have known' (P 165). In other words, the practice of morality forces the idea of freedom upon us. But,

Kant argues, this idea, viewed theoretically, contains a contradiction, and he displays this contradiction in the third antinomy of the first *Critique*.

Every change which occurs in the order of nature has a cause: this is an 'established principle' of the Analytic, and 'allows of no exception' (A 536, B 564). If this is so, then every event in nature is bound in chains of ineluctable necessity. At the same time I think of myself as the originator of my actions, giving rise to them spontaneously, under the influence of no external constraint. If my action is part of nature, this seems to contradict the view that every event in nature is bound by causal necessity. If it is not part of nature, then it falls outside the realm of causal connection, and my will is the originator of nothing in the natural world.

There is only a contradiction here if I really *am* free. Kant is sometimes content to argue merely that I must *think* of myself as free. It is a presupposition of all action in the world – and hence of reasoned decisions – that the agent is the originator of what he does. And, Kant suggests, I cannot forsake this idea without losing the sense of myself as agent. The very perspective of reason which sees the world as bound in chains of necessity also sees it as containing freedom. Occasionally Kant goes further, and argues for the 'primacy' of practical reason (P 313f.), meaning that *all* thought is an exercise of freedom, so that, if practical reason were impossible, we could not think coherently. In which case the certainty of my freedom is as great as the certainty of anything. (This argument occurs, in more rhetorical form, in the writings of Sartre, whose existentialist doctrine of the moral life owes much to Kant.) If this is true, then of course the antinomy of freedom becomes acute: we are compelled by practical reason to accept that we are free, and by understanding to deny it.

Kant felt that there must be a solution to this antinomy, since in the practical sphere the employment of reason is legitimate. It is indeed practical reason which tells me what I am. The illusory progress of *pure* reason towards self-contradiction ought not to forbid *practical* reason, through which the antinomy must therefore be resolved. Pure reason leaves, as it were, a 'vacant place' in its account of the world, where the moral agent should be. 'This vacant place is filled by pure practical reason with a definite law of causality in an intelligible world . . . namely, the moral law' (P 195). This new 'law of causality' is called 'transcendental freedom', and it defines the condition of the moral agent. The law of cause and effect operates only in the realm of nature (the empirical realm). Freedom, however, belongs, not to nature, but precisely to that 'intelligible' or transcendental realm to which categories like causality do not apply. I exist in the world of nature, as one 'appearance' among others. But I also exist as a 'thing-in-itself', bound not by causality, but by the laws of practical reason. It is not that I am *two* things, but rather one thing, conceived under two contrasting aspects. Thus 'there is not the smallest contradiction in saying that a *thing in appearance* (belonging to the world of sense) is subject to certain laws, from which the very same as a *thing in itself* is independent'. Moreover the moral agent must always 'conceive and think of himself in this two-fold way' (F 112). Freedom, then, is a transcendental 'idea', without application in the empirical world. And in knowing ourselves to be free we know ourselves at the same time as part of nature and as members of a transcendental world.

The transcendental self

The doctrine of transcendental freedom is both puzzling and appealing. Its appeal lies in its promise of access to the transcendental; its puzzling quality comes from Kant's previous proof that such access is impossible. By Kant's own argument, there is nothing to be known, and nothing meaningfully to be said, about the transcendental world. Kant recognises the difficulty, and admits that the 'demand to regard oneself *qua* subject of freedom as a noumenon, and at the same time from the point of view of physical nature as a phenomenon in one's own empirical consciousness' is 'paradoxical' (P 130). And he even goes so far as to say that, while we do not comprehend the fact of moral freedom, 'we yet comprehend its *incomprehensibility*, and this is all that can fairly be demanded of a philosophy which strives to carry its principles to the very limit of human reason' (F 122).

We can go some way towards explaining Kant's doctrine if we relate the 'transcendental freedom' that underlies practical reason to the 'transcendental unity of apperception' which underlies our knowledge of nature. Our perspective on the world contains two distinct aspects; and neither the unity of consciousness, nor transcendental freedom, can be deduced from our knowledge of the empirical world. But they are each guaranteed a priori as preconditions of the knowledge which we have. The first is the starting-point for all our knowledge of truths, the second the starting-point for all deliberation. They are transcendental, not in the positive sense of involving knowledge of a transcendental object, but in the negative sense of lying at the limit of what can be known. Freedom, being a perspective *on* the empirical world, cannot also be part of it. The knowledge of our own freedom is therefore a part of the 'apperception' which defines our perspective. (Authority for this interpretation can be found in the first *Critique*, notably A 546–7, B 574–5.)

Pure reason attempts to know the transcendental world through concepts. In other words, it attempts to form a positive conception of noumena. This attempt is doomed to failure. Practical reason, however, not being concerned in the discovery of truths, imposes no concepts on its objects. It will never, therefore, lead us into the error of forming a positive conception of the transcendental self. We know this self only practically, through the exercise of freedom. While we cannot translate this knowledge into judgements about our nature, we can translate it into some other thing. This other thing is given by the laws of practical reason, which are the synthetic a priori principles of action. Just as there are a priori laws of nature that can be derived from the unity of consciousness, so too are there a priori laws of reason which can be derived from the perspective of transcendental freedom. These will not be laws about the true and the false: they will have no part to play in description, prediction and explanation. They will be practical laws, concerning what to do. The free agent will be bound by them in all his practical reasoning, since acceptance of them is a presupposition of the freedom without which practical reason is impossible.

It is true that Kant wavers between the doctrine that the transcendental self is a kind of perspective, and the doctrine that it is a distinct noumenal thing. He even attempts to resuscitate through practical reason all those theoretical conclusions concerning God, the soul and immortality that had been dismissed as illusions of pure reason. I shall not, for the present, follow Kant into these mysterious regions. But the reader should bear in mind that I have only postponed the deep metaphysical problem which Kant's ethical doctrine creates.

The problem of practical reason

Kant's idea of freedom becomes clearer when seen in the context of the problem that it was supposed to solve. Rational beings exist not only as self-conscious centres of knowledge, but also as agents. Their reason is not detached from their agency, but forms a constitutive part of it; which is to say that, for a rational being there is not only action, but also the *question* of action (the question 'What shall I do?'), and this question demands a reasoned answer. My rationality is expressed in the fact that some of my actions are intentional (they issue, to use Kant's term, from my 'will'). Of all such actions the question can be asked: Why do that? This question asks, not for a cause or explanation, but for a reason. Suppose someone asks me why I struck an old man in the street. The answer: 'Because electrical impulses from my brain precipitated muscular contractions, and this resulted in my hand making contact with his head' would be absurd and impertinent, however accurate as a causal explanation. The answer: 'Because he annoyed me' may be inadequate, in that it gives no good reason, but it is certainly not absurd. Reasons are designed to justify action, and not primarily to explain it. They refer to the grounds of an action, the premises from which an agent may conclude what to do.

Practical reasons concern either ends or means. If I have an end in view then I may deliberate over the means to achieve it. All philosophers agree that such reasoning exists; but many of them think that it shows no special 'practical' employment of the rational faculties. It is merely theoretical reason, put to use. Kant himself is of this view, arguing that 'precepts of skill' (how to find the means to one's ends) are merely theoretical principles (P 157). Sceptical philosophers go further, and argue, with Hume, that there is no other use for reason in practical matters. All reasoning concerns means. Reason can neither generate, nor justify, the ends of our activity, since, in Hume's words, 'reason is, and ought to be, the slave of the passions'. It is from the 'passions' that our ends are drawn, since it is passion, and passion only, that provides the ultimate motive to act. Reason can persuade us to act only when we are already motivated to obey it. If that is the case, then, Kant held, there can be no objective practical knowledge. For there can be no way in which reason will settle the question what to do.

Kant held that practical reason is possible. He affirmed the (common-sense) belief that reason may constrain and justify not only the choice of means, but also the choice of ends upon which it depends. In which case there may be an objective exercise of practical reason. It would be objective because based in reason alone, recommending ends of action to any rational being, irrespective of his passions, interests and desires. For this to be possible, however, reason must, as Hume argued, not only justify but also motivate our actions. If reason did not also *prompt* me to act, then reason would play no part in the process of decision-making. So it would not be practical. Now, if reason generates only judgements about the world and inferences therefrom, it is hard to see how it *can* be a motive to act. That such and such a judgement is true or false may prompt me to all kinds of action, depending upon my ends. If these ends stem from the 'passions' then reason has no part in determining them. The only way in which reason can become practical, therefore, is by issuing not in judgements but in imperatives. An imperative does not describe the world; it addresses itself to an agent, and, if he accepts it, determines what he does. If, therefore, there are imperatives which arise simply from the exercise of reason, then reason alone can move us to action. 'Reason, with its practical law, determines the will immediately' (P 156).

Autonomy of the will

Kant's moral philosophy emerges from the amalgamation of the idea of transcendental freedom with that of an imperative of reason. He believes that reasoning about ends must always suppose just the kind of transcendental freedom that his metaphysics claims to be possible. Freedom is the power to will an end of action for myself. Any derivation of my ends from an external source is at the same time a subjection of myself to that source. And any natural process which governs my action confers on me the unfreedom of its cause. I then become the passive channel through which natural forces find their enactment. If my action is called unfree it is because there is a sense in which it is not truly *mine*.

An action that originates in me can be attributed *only* to me, and is therefore in a real sense mine. In respect of such an action I am free. I act freely whenever *I* act, and unfreely whenever some other agency acts through me. This raises the question what am *I*? The obvious answer is 'a transcendental self'; since that explains my freedom from the causality of nature. But Kant now supplements this answer with a theory of the will. An action originates in me whenever I decide on the action, simply on the basis of considering *it*. I do not consult my desires, interest or any other 'empirical condition', since that is to subject myself to the causality of nature. I simply reflect on the action, and choose it for its own sake, as an end in itself. This is the paradigm of a free action: one that is brought into being by reason alone. Such an action can be attributed, Kant thought, to no 'natural' force, no chain of 'empirical' causality. It arises spontaneously out of the rational processes which constitute my will.

Freedom, then, is the ability to be governed by reason. The imperatives of reason discussed in the last section are 'laws of freedom': principles whereby reason determines action. So that there is a 'causality of freedom' in addition to the 'causality of nature', and freedom is nothing more than obedience to the first, perhaps in defiance of the second. This ability to be motivated by reason alone Kant called the autonomy of the will, and he contrasted it with the 'heteronomy' of the agent whose will is subject to external causes. Kant designates as external any cause which belongs to the 'causality of nature' – that is, any cause which is not founded in reason alone. An action which springs from desire, emotion or interest is therefore 'heteronomous'.

Kant now develops his conception of the autonomous *agent*. This is an agent who is able to overcome the promptings of all heteronomous counsels, such as those of self-interest and desire, should they be in conflict with reason. Such a being postulates himself as a 'transcendental being', in that he defies the causality of nature and refers the grounds of his actions always to the 'causality of freedom'. Only an autonomous being has genuine ends of action (as opposed to mere objects of desire), and only such a being deserves our esteem, as the embodiment of rational choice. The autonomy of the will, Kant goes on to argue, 'is the sole principle of all moral laws, and of all duties which conform to them; on the other hand, heteronomy of the will not only cannot be the basis of any obligation, but is, on the contrary, opposed to the principle thereof, and to the morality of will' (P 169). Because autonomy is manifest only in the obedience to reason, and because reason must guide action always through imperatives, autonomy is described as 'that property of the will whereby it is a law to itself' (F 85).

Metaphysical difficulties

We must now return to the metaphysical problem of transcendental freedom. Two difficulties in particular stand out, since they correspond to difficulties which Kant himself had discovered in the rationalist metaphysics of Leibniz. First, how is the transcendental self to be individuated? What makes *this* self *me*? If the essential feature is reason and the agency which springs from it, then, since the laws of reason are universal, how am I to be distinguished from any other being who is subject to them? If the essential feature is my 'point of view' on the world, how is Kant to avoid the Leibnizian view of the self as a monad, defined by its point of view, but existing outside the world that it 'represents' thereby, incapable of entering into real relation with anything contained in it?

Secondly (or rather to continue the objection), how is the transcendental self related to the empirical world? In particular, how is it related to its own action, which is either an event in the empirical world or else totally ineffective? I must exist, as Kant acknowledges, both as an 'empirical self', within the realm of nature, and as a transcendental self, outside it. But since the category of cause applies only to nature, the transcendental self remains for ever ineffective. In which case, why is its freedom so valuable? Kant relies on the view that the category of cause denotes a relation in time (of before and after); whereas the relation of a reason to that which springs from it is not temporal at all (P 269). His tortuous discussion of this in the first *Critique* (A 538–41, B 566–9) fails to make clear how a reason offered to the transcendental self can motivate (and so explain) an event in the empirical world.

Kant's preferred stance towards these difficulties is summarised in the assertion that the idea of ourselves as members of a purely 'intelligible' realm to which categories do not apply 'remains always a useful and legitimate idea for the purpose of rational belief, although all knowledge stops at its threshold' (F 121). At the same time, Kant continued to regard the paradox of human freedom as unavoidable: we could never solve it through theoretical reason, while practical reason assured us only that it *has* a solution. However, we must acknowledge 'the right of pure reason in its practical use to an extension which is not possible in its speculative use' (P 197). Hence we can accept the verdict of practical reason on trust. Of course, we can always raise the question of freedom anew: it then becomes 'How is practical reason possible?' We know that it *is* possible, for without it our perspective on the world would vanish. But 'how pure reason can be practical – to explain this is beyond the power of human reason' (F 119).

Kant is able to derive, with compelling logic, an entire system of common-sense morality from the premise of transcendental freedom. Since the paradox of freedom remains unsolved at the end of this derivation, Kant may not be wholly wrong in his suggestion that we shall never be able to comprehend it.

Hypothetical and categorical imperatives

There is a division in practical thought between hypothetical and categorical imperatives. The first typically begin with an 'If . . .', as in 'If you want to stay, be polite!' Here the end is hypothetical, and the imperative states the means to it. The validity of all such imperatives can be established in accordance with the 'supreme principle' that 'whoever wills the end, wills the means'. This principle, Kant argues, is analytic (it derives its truth from concepts alone). But, although hypothetical imperatives may be valid, they can never be objective, since they are always *conditional*. They give a reason only to the person who has the end mentioned in the antecedent (in the example given above, the person who wants to stay), and are binding on no one whose desires conflict with it. This is true even of the 'counsels of prudence', which tell us what to do in order to be happy. For the concept of happiness is merely a label for whatever a rational being desires; the hypothetical imperatives which refer us to our happiness apply universally only because they specify nothing determinate. One man's happiness may be another's pain, and the imperative accepted by one may not recommend itself to the other. It seems then that all hypothetical imperatives remain subjective, conditional on the individual's desires, and none of them corresponds to a true 'command of reason'.

Categorical imperatives do not typically contain an 'if'. They tell you what to do *unconditionally*. They may nevertheless be defended by reasons. If I say 'Shut the door!' then my command is arbitrary unless I can answer the question 'Why?' If I answer it to your satisfaction, then the imperative binds you. If the answer refers to some independent interest of yours, however, the imperative also ceases to be categorical, as in 'If you want to avoid punishment, shut the door.' Only if the answer represents the action *itself* as an end do we have a non-arbitrary categorical imperative. The signal of this is the presence of an 'ought': 'You ought to shut the door'. In the categorical 'ought' we have the true imperative of reason.

It is not implausible to follow Kant in aligning this familiar distinction between hypothetical and categorical imperatives with the distinction between reasoning over means and reasoning over ends. The problem of practical reason then becomes 'How are categorical imperatives possible?' Furthermore, Kant argues, morality can be expressed only in categorical imperatives. 'If duty is a conception that is to have any import and real legislative authority for our actions, it can only be expressed in categorical imperatives and not at all in hypothetical imperatives' (F 60). Obedience to a hypothetical imperative is always obedience to the condition expressed in its antecedent. It therefore always involves heteronomy of the will. Obedience to a categorical imperative, however, since it springs from reason alone, must always be autonomous. Thus Kant also aligns the distinction between the two kinds of imperatives with that between heteronomy and autonomy, and thereby associates the problem of the categorical imperatives with that of transcendental freedom: 'what makes categorical imperatives possible is this, that the idea of freedom makes me a member of an intelligible world' (F 107).

But if categorical imperatives are to be possible, they too require a supreme principle, which will show how reason discovers them. Hence practical reason is faced with a problem as general as the problem of theoretical reason, and requiring the same kind of answer. We must show how synthetic a priori *practical* knowledge is possible. The supreme principle of hypothetical imperatives is, as we have seen, analytic. Hence hypothetical imperatives make no real demands on the agent, but simply relate his ends to the means needed to secure them. Categorical imperatives, however, make real and unconditional demands: they are, in that sense, synthetic. Moreover, since their foundation lies in reason alone, they must be based a priori. The very form of a categorical imperative prevents it from deriving authority from any other source – for example, from a desire, need or interest, or any other 'empirical condition' of the agent. In particular, there is no way in which categorical imperatives can be deduced from 'the particular attributes of human nature' (F 61). Thus Kant rejects all the usual systems of ethics of his day, arguing that they are unable to explain, what alone upholds the objectivity of moral judgement, the 'unconditional necessity' which attaches to the moral law. This necessity is explained only by a theory with an a priori basis. Hence all reference to empirical conditions – even to the most established facts of human nature – must be excluded from the grounds of morality (F 64).

The categorical imperative

The supreme principle of categorical imperatives is called *the* categorical imperative, on the assumption that there is, or ought to be, only one such principle (perhaps to avoid the possibility of conflicting duties (L 20)). In fact the principle is restated in five variant forms, two of which involve new conceptions. It is therefore normal to consider the categorical imperative as a composite law of reason, with three separate parts. The law is derived, in its first and most famous formulation, as follows.

If we are to find an imperative that recommends itself on the basis of reason alone, then we must abstract from all the distinctions between rational agents, discounting their interests, desires and ambitions, and all the 'empirical conditions' which circumscribe their actions. Only then will we base our law in practical reason alone, since we will have abstracted from any other ground. By this process of abstraction I arrive at the 'point of view of a member of an intelligible world' (F 108). This is a point of view outside my own experience, which could therefore be adopted by any rational being, whatever his circumstances. The law that I formulate will then be an imperative that applies universally, to all rational beings. When deciding on my action as an end, I will be constrained by reason to 'act only on that maxim which I can at the same time will as a universal law' (my paraphrase from F 38). (The term 'maxim' means both 'principle' and 'motive': a categorical imperative always commands, and always lays down a law.) The principle is in one sense 'formal': that is, it commands nothing specific. At the same time it is synthetic, since it legislates among all the possible ends of action, allowing some, and forbidding others. For example, it forbids the breaking of promises, for to will the universal breaking of promises is to will the abolition of promising, hence to will the abolition of the advantage which accrues to breaking promises, and so to will the abolition of my motive. Such forbidden ends of action are shown, by their confrontation with the supreme moral law, to involve the agent in a contradiction.

Kant regarded this first formulation of the categorical imperative as the philosophical basis of the famous golden rule, that we should do as we would be done by. It is a priori in that it is based in what can recommend itself to reason alone. This explains its right to a 'universal' form, and to the kind of necessity embodied in the categorical 'ought'.

The categorical imperative finds the ends of action by abstracting from everything but the fact of rational agency. Rational agency must therefore provide its own ends. The autonomous being is both the agent and the repository of all value, and exists, as Kant puts it (F 65), 'as an end in himself'. If we are to have values at all, we must value (respect) the existence and endeavours of rational beings. In this way autonomy prescribes its own limit. The constraint on our freedom is that we must respect the freedom of all: how else can our freedom issue in *universal* laws? It follows that we must never use another without regard to his autonomy; we must never treat him as a means. This brings us to the second major formulation of the categorical imperative, as the law that I must 'so act as to treat humanity, whether in my own self or in that of another, always as an end, and never as a means only' (my paraphrase from F 47). 'Humanity' here covers all rational beings, and the distinction between those beings which can and those which cannot be regarded as mere means, is what we are referring to in distinguishing *things* from *persons*. This distinction is the foundation of the concept of a 'right'. If someone asks whether an animal, a child or an inanimate object has rights, he is asking whether the categorical imperative applies to it, in this second, most powerful, form.

We cannot, then, treat rational agents merely as the means through which external forces find enactment: to do so is to deny the autonomy which alone commands our respect. In abstracting towards the moral law, I am always respecting the sovereignty of reason. So while the form of my law is universal (the first imperative), its content must derive from its application to rational beings as ends in themselves (the second imperative). Hence I must always think of the moral law as a piece of universal legislation, which binds rational beings equally. I am thereby led to the idea of 'the will of every rational being as a universally legislative will' (F 70). This conception in turn leads to another, that of a 'kingdom of ends', in which the universal legislation to which we all willingly bow when acting autonomously has become a law of nature. So 'every rational being must so act as if he were by his maxims in every case a legislating member of the universal kingdom of ends' (my paraphrase from F 49–50). This third imperative suggests that all speculation about ends is also the postulation of an ideal world, in which things are as they ought to be and ought to be as they are. In this kingdom nothing conflicts with reason, and the rational being is both subject and sovereign of the law which there obtains.

Moral intuitions

Kant believes that the various formulations of the categorical imperative can be derived by reflection on the single idea of autonomy, and that this alone is sufficient to recommend them to every rational being. He also thinks that they lend support to ordinary moral thought, just as the synthetic a priori principles of the understanding uphold our common scientific knowledge. It is a singular merit of Kant's moral system that it imposes order on an intuitive vision of morality. This vision is not the property of one man only, but (as Kant and many others have thought) of all people everywhere. Kant had been much influenced by the third Lord Shaftesbury (1671–1713) and his followers – the so-called 'British Moralists' – who had argued that certain fundamental moral principles were not matters of individual preference, but rather, when reduced to their true basis in the human soul, universally acceptable, recording the unspoken agreement of rational beings everywhere. Kant accepted that view. But he attempted to free it from the study of our 'niggardly stepmother', nature (F 10). It was of the greatest importance to him, therefore, that his theory should generate the axioms of an intuitive morality. 'We have simply showed by the development of the universally received notion of morality that an autonomy of the will is inevitably connected with it' (F 92). It is instructive to list some of the common intuitions which Kant's theory explains.

(*i*) *The content of morality.* Common morality enjoins respect for others and for oneself; it forbids exceptions in one's own favour; it regards all men as equal before the moral law. These are immediate consequences of the categorical imperative. In its second formulation, moreover, the imperative lends support to quite specific, and universally accepted, laws. It forbids murder, rape, theft, fraud and dishonesty, along with all forms of arbitrary compulsion. It imposes a universal duty to respect the rights and interests of others, and a rational requirement to abstract from personal involvement towards the viewpoint of the impartial judge. Thus it encapsulates fundamental intuitions about justice, together with a specific and intuitively acceptable moral code.

(*ii*) *The force of morality.* On Kant's view, the motive of morality is quite different from that of interest or desire. It rules us absolutely and necessarily, we feel its power even when we are most defying it. It is not one consideration to be balanced against others, but rather a compelling dictate which can be ignored but never refuted. This accords, he thinks, with common intuition. If a man is told that he can satisfy the greatest of his lusts, only on condition that he will afterwards be hanged, then he is sure to refuse the offer. But if he is told that he must betray his friend, bear false witness, kill an innocent, or else be hanged, then his interest in his own life counts for nothing in determining what he ought to do. He may bow to the threat; but only with a consciousness of doing wrong; and the moral law itself, unlike any motive of desire, propels him onward to destruction.

(iii) The good will. In the moral judgement of action we refer the consequences produced to the agent who produced them. Unlike the intentional or the negligent the unforeseeable and unintended is never blamed. Moral judgement is directed, not to the effects of an action, but to the good or bad intention that it shows. Hence, in Kant's famous words, 'nothing can possibly be conceived in the world, or even out of it, which can be called good without qualification, except a good will' (F 11). Kant's theory accords exactly with this common intuition. All virtue is contained in autonomy, all vice in its absence, and all morality is summarised in the imperatives that guide the will.

(iv) The moral agent. Underlying intuitive morality is a view of the moral agent. The moral agent is differently motivated and differently constituted from the agencies of nature. His actions have not only causes, but also reasons. He makes decisions for the future, and so distinguishes his intentions from his desires. He does not suffer his desires always to overcome him, but sometimes resists and subdues them. In everything he is both active and passive, and stands as legislator among his own emotions. The moral agent is an object not only of affection and love (which we may extend to all of nature) but also of esteem, and he commands our esteem to the extent that the moral law is manifest in him. In all these intuitive distinctions – between reason and cause, intention and desire, action and passion, esteem and affection – we find aspects of the vital distinction which underlies them, that between person and thing. Only a person has rights, duties and obligations; only a person acts for reasons in addition to causes; only a person merits our esteem. The philosophy of the categorical imperative explains this distinction and all those which reflect it. It also explains why the

'respect for persons' lies embedded in every moral code.

(*v*) *The role of law*. Someone may act as the good man acts, but this casts no credit on him if his motive is self-interest. We distinguish action *according to* duty from action *from* duty, and confine our praise to the second. 'The former (*legality*) is possible even if inclinations have been the determining principles of the will; but the latter (*morality*) has moral value, which can be placed only in this: that the action is done out of duty ...' (P 248). This is a clear and intuitively acceptable consequence of Kant's theory. So too is the more theoretical proposition, that the fundamental concept in moral thought is not goodness, but obligation (P 217).

(*vi*) *Reason and the passions*. We recognise in all our moral efforts that there may be a conflict between duty and desire. There thus arises, in every moral being, the idea of conscience as an independent motive, able to legislate among desires and so to forbid or permit them. Kant distinguishes the 'good will' of the moral agent from the 'holy will' that acts always without resistance from desire. The 'holy will' needs no imperative (P 168) since it bends automatically in the direction of duty, whereas the ordinary agent stands always in need of principles, since his inclination is to thwart them. This sense of the conflict between reason and the passions is a widespread intuition. Kant takes it, however, to somewhat counter-intuitive extremes. He believes that the motive of benevolence, so dear to empiricist morality, is a species of mere inclination, and therefore morally neutral. 'It is a very beautiful thing to do good to men from love to them and from sympathetic goodwill, or to be just from love of order, but this is not the true moral maxim' (P 249). Kant seems to have more praise for the misanthropy which does good against every inclination, than for the expressions of cheerful benevolence. It is in his ability to *resist* inclination that the worth of the moral agent resides. When, for example, a man who desires death goes on living out of a duty of self-preservation, only then, and for the first time, does self-preservation, in ceasing to be an instinct, become a sign of moral worth.

Morality and the self

Those intuitions already lead us, Kant thinks, towards the doctrine of a transcendental freedom. If that doctrine is nonsense, then so is all our moral and practical thought. For if we examine the intuitions systematically, we see that they distinguish the moral agent from his desires, and the free, reason-governed, autonomous nature of the person, from the unfree, passive (or, in Kant's term, 'pathological') nature of the animal. Surely, then, we must face up to the paradox of freedom. For we do think of ourselves both as empirical beings, bound by the laws of causality, and as transcendental beings, obedient to imperatives of reason alone.

We must remind ourselves again of the methodological character of the 'transcendental object'. This phrase designates, not an object of knowledge, but a limit to knowledge, defined by the perspective of practical reason. I am constrained by reason to view the world as a 'field of action', and hence to postulate the freedom of my will. Only from that postulate can I deliberate at all. From this perspective of practical reason I arrive inexorably at the categorical imperatives which compel my action. On one interpretation the doctrine of the self and its agency is not a doctrine of how things *are* in a transcendental world, but of how things *seem* in the empirical world. 'The conception of an intelligible world is then only a *point of view* which reason finds itself compelled to take outside appearances, *in order to conceive itself as practical*' (F 114). The rational agent requires, then, a special perspective on the world: he sees his actions under the aspect of freedom, and while what he sees is the same as what he sees when studying the world scientifically, his practical knowledge cannot be expressed in scientific terms. He seeks not causes but reasons, not mechanisms but rational ends, not descriptive laws but imperatives. Thus Kant answers in the affirmative the question posed in the first *Critique*: 'is it possible to regard one and the same event as being in one aspect merely an effect of nature and in another aspect due to freedom?' (A 543, B 571). But the answer, referring as it does to a transcendental perspective, is such that we can comprehend only its incomprehensibility (F 122).

The objectivity of morals

If my freedom and the laws which guide it are constituted by a particular way things seem, how can I consider the commands of morality to be objectively valid? Reason alone, Kant argues, compels me to accept the categorical imperative; hence it has 'objective necessity'. It does not matter that this compulsion issues from a point of view. For the same is true of the compulsion to accept the a priori laws of science. If reason is both a motive to action, and also impelled by its nature towards definite precepts, what more can be demanded by way of objectivity? When someone asks 'Why should I be moral?' he is asking for a reason. An answer that refers to his interests binds him only 'conditionally'. But the perspective of practical reason is able to rise above all 'conditions', and this is part of what is implied in its 'transcendental' nature. It generates imperatives which bind unconditionally. In which case it answers the question 'Why be moral?' for all rational agents, irrespective of their desires. The man with evil desires can no more escape the force of reason's answer than the man who desires what is right.

So conceived, the task of proving the objectivity of morality is less great than that of proving the objectivity of science, despite popular prejudice to the contrary. For the faculty of the understanding requires two 'deductions', one to show what we must believe, the other to show what is true. Practical reason, which makes no claims to truth, does not stand in need of this second, 'objective', deduction. It is enough that reason compels us to think according to the categorical imperative. There is nothing further to be proved about an independent world. If sometimes we speak of moral truth, and moral reality, this is but another way of referring to the constraints which reason places on our conduct.

The moral life

The moral nature of the rational being resides in his ability to impregnate all his judgements, motives and affections with the universal demands of practical reason. Even in our most private and intimate encounters, reason covertly abstracts from the immediate circumstances and reminds us of the moral law. Those philosophers – such as Shaftesbury, Hutcheson and Hume – who had stressed the importance to morality of the emotions, were not wrong, except in their faulty concept of emotion. The moral life involves the exercise of anger, remorse, indignation, pride, esteem and respect. And these are all emotions, since they are not subject to the will. '*Respect* is a *tribute* which we cannot refuse to merit, whether we will or not; we may indeed outwardly withhold it, but we cannot help feeling it inwardly' (P 241). But at the heart of such emotions is a respect for the moral law, and an abstraction from present and immediate conditions. It is this which justifies their place in the moral life of rational beings. Kant's discussion of pride and self-respect (L 120–7) is remarkably acute. By emphasising the element of reason that lies embedded in human emotion, he is able to rebut the charge that 'moral feeling' plays no part in the motivation of the rational man (L 139). But any theory which pays attention to the complexity of moral feeling must emphasise the imperative which lies at its heart.

The process of abstraction leads us, Kant thought, in a metaphysical direction. The moral life imposes an intimation of transcendental reality; we feel compelled towards the belief in God, in immortality, and in a divine ordinance in nature. These 'postulates of practical reason' are as ineluctable a product of moral thought as the imperative which guides us. Pure reason falls over itself in the attempt to prove the existence of God and the immortality of the soul. But 'from the practical point of view the *possibility* [of these doctrines] must be assumed, although we cannot theoretically know and understand it' (P 127). This obscure concession to the claims of theology is hard to accept. But some light is cast on Kant's intention by the third of his *Critiques*, to the examination of which we now must turn.

6 Beauty and design

It is not God's command that binds us to morality, but morality that points to the possibility of a 'holy will'. Kant warns against the 'fanaticism, indeed the impiety, of abandoning the guidance of a morally legislative reason in the right conduct of our lives, in order to derive guidance directly from the idea of the Supreme Being' (A 819, B 847). Kant's writings on religion exhibit one of the first attempts at the systematic demystification of theology. He criticises all forms of anthropomorphism, and expounds, in his *Religion Within the Limits of Reason Alone* (1793), a 'hermeneutical rule' of 'moral interpretation'. All scripture and religious doctrine that conflicts with reason must be interpreted allegorically, so as to express moral insights which gain vivacity, rather than validity, from their religious expression. The attempt to make the idea of God intelligible through images, and so to subsume God under the categories of the empirical world, is self-contradictory. If God is a transcendental being, then there is nothing to be said of him from our point of view except that he transcends it. If he is not a transcendental being, then he no more deserves our respect than any other work of nature. Under the first interpretation we can respect him only because we respect the moral law which points towards his existence. On the second interpretation, we could respect him only as a subject of the moral law which governs his activity.

Kant's demythologised religion was not uncommon among his contemporaries. He differed, however, in appropriating the images of traditional religion for the veneration of morality. The worship due to God becomes reverence and devotion for the moral law. The faith which transcends belief becomes the certainty of practical reason which surpasses understanding. The object of esteem is not the Supreme Being, but the supreme attribute of rationality. The moral world is described as the 'realm of grace' (A 815, B 844), the actual community of rational beings as the 'mystical body' in the world of nature (A 808, B 836), and the Kingdom of God to which mortals aspire is transmuted into the Kingdom of Ends which they make real through their self-legislation. It is not surprising to learn from one of Jachmann's letters that 'many evangelists went forth [from Kant's lectures on theology] and preached the gospel of the Kingdom of Reason'.

Nevertheless, Kant accepted the traditional claims of theology, and even tried to resuscitate them under the obscure doctrine of the 'postulates of practical reason'. Moreover, he felt that one of the traditional arguments for God's existence, the argument from design, contains a vital clue to the nature of creation. It is in the third *Critique*, at the end of an account of aesthetic experience, that Kant attempts to reveal his meaning.

The Third Critique

The *Critique of Judgement* is a disorganised and repetitious work, which gains little from Kant's struggle to impose on its somewhat diffuse subject-matter the structure of the transcendental philosophy. A contemporary who attended Kant's lectures on aesthetics recorded that 'the principal thoughts of his *Critique of Judgement* [were] given as easily, clearly, and entertainingly as can be imagined'. Kant was seventy-one when he came to write the work, however, and there seems little doubt that his mastery of argument and of the written word were beginning to desert him. Nevertheless, the third *Critique* is one of the most important works of aesthetics to have been composed in modern times; indeed, it could fairly be said that, were it not for this work, aesthetics would not exist in its modern form. Kant's most feeble arguments were here used to present some of his most original conclusions.

Kant felt the need to explore in the *Critique of Judgement* certain questions left over from the first two *Critiques*. Moreover he wished to provide for aesthetics its own 'faculty', corresponding to understanding and practical reason. The faculty of judgement 'mediates' between the other two. It enables us to see the empirical world as conforming to the ends of practical reason, and practical reason as adapted to our knowledge of the empirical world. Kant believed that 'judgement' has both a subjective and an objective aspect, and divided his *Critique* accordingly. The first part, concerned with the subjective experience of 'purposiveness' or 'finality', is devoted to aesthetic judgement. The second, concerned with the objective 'finality' of nature, is devoted to the natural manifestation of design. I shall concentrate on the first, which suffices in itself to bring the critical system to its conclusion.

The eighteenth century saw the birth of modern aesthetics. Shaftesbury and his followers made penetrating observations on the experience of beauty; Burke presented his famous distinction between the beautiful and the sublime; Batteux in France and Lessing and Winckelmann in Germany attempted to provide universal principles for the classification and judgement of works of art. The Leibnizians also made their contribution, and the modern use of the term 'aesthetic' is due to Kant's mentor A. G. Baumgarten. Nevertheless, no philosopher since Plato had given to aesthetic experience the central role in philosophy that Kant was to give to it. Nor had Kant's predecessors perceived, as he perceived, that both metaphysics and ethics must remain incomplete without a theory of the aesthetic. Only a rational being can experience beauty; and without the experience of beauty, rationality is unfulfilled. It is only in the aesthetic experience of nature, Kant suggests, that we grasp the relation of our faculties to the world, and so understand both our own limitations, and the possibility of transcending them. Aesthetic experience intimates to us that our point of view is, after all, only *our* point of view, and that we are no more creators of nature than we are creators of the point of view from which we observe and act on it. Momentarily we stand outside that point of view, not so as to have knowledge of a transcendent world, but so as to perceive the harmony that exists between our faculties and the objects in relation to which they are employed. At the same time we sense the divine order that makes this harmony possible.

The problem of beauty

Kant's aesthetics is based on a fundamental problem, which he expresses in many different forms, eventually giving to it the structure of an 'antinomy'. According to the 'antinomy of taste' aesthetic judgement seems to be in conflict with itself: it cannot be at the same time aesthetic (an expression of subjective experience) and also a judgement (claiming universal assent). And yet all rational beings, simply in virtue of their rationality, seem disposed to make these judgements. On the one hand, they feel pleasure in an object, and this pleasure is immediate, not based in any conceptualisation of the object, or in any inquiry into cause, purpose or constitution. On the other hand they express their pleasure in the form of a judgement, speaking 'as if beauty were a quality of the object' (J 51), thus representing their pleasure as objectively valid. But how can this be so? The pleasure is immediate, based in no reasoning or analysis; so what permits this demand for universal agreement?

However we approach the idea of beauty we find this paradox emerging. Our attitudes, feelings and judgements are called aesthetic precisely because of their direct relation to experience. Hence no one can judge the beauty of an object that he has never heard or seen. Scientific judgements, like practical principles, can be received 'at second hand'. I can take you as my authority for the truths of physics, or for the utility of trains. But I cannot take you as my authority for the merits of Leonardo, or for the beauties of Mozart, if I have seen no work by the one or heard none by the other. It would seem to follow from this that there can be no rules or principles of aesthetic judgement. 'A principle of taste would mean a fundamental premise under the condition of which one might subsume the concept of an object, and then, by a syllogism, draw the inference that it is beautiful. That, however, is absolutely impossible. For I must feel the pleasure immediately in the perception of the object, and I cannot be talked into it by any grounds of proof' (J 141). It seems that it is always experience, and never conceptual thought, that gives the right to aesthetic judgement, so that anything which alters the experience of an object alters its aesthetic significance (which is why poetry cannot be translated). As Kant puts it, aesthetic judgement is 'free from concepts', and beauty itself is not a concept. Hence we arrive at the first proposition of the antinomy of taste: 'The judgement of taste is not based on concepts; for, if it were, it would be open to dispute (decision by means of proofs)' (J 198).

However, such a conclusion seems to be inconsistent with the fact that aesthetic judgement is a form of *judgement*. When I describe something as beautiful I do not mean merely that it pleases *me*: I am speaking about it, not about myself, and if challenged I try to find reasons for my view. I do not *explain* my feeling, but give *grounds* for it, by pointing to features of its object. And any search for reasons has the universal character of rationality. I am in effect saying that others, in so far as they are rational, ought to feel just the same delight as I feel. This points to the second proposition of Kant's antinomy: 'the judgement of taste is based on concepts; for otherwise ... there could be no room even for contention in the matter, or for the claim to the necessary agreement of others' (J 198).

The synthetic a priori grounds of taste

Kant says that the judgement of beauty is grounded not in concepts but in a feeling of pleasure; at the same time this pleasure is postulated as universally valid, and even 'necessary'. The aesthetic judgement contains an 'ought': others ought to feel as I do, and to the extent that they do not, either they or I am wrong. It is this which leads us to seek reasons for our judgements. The terms 'universality' and 'necessity' refer us to the defining properties of the a priori. It is clear that the postulate that others ought to feel as I do is not derived from experience: it is, on the contrary, a presupposition of aesthetic pleasure. Nor is it analytic. Hence its status must be synthetic a priori.

The argument is very slippery. The 'necessity' of the judgement of taste has little to do with the necessity of the a priori laws of the understanding, nor does its universality issue in a definite principle. Kant sometimes recognises this, and speaks of aesthetic *pleasure* rather than aesthetic judgement as universally valid, and so a priori (J 146). Nevertheless, he was convinced that aesthetics raises precisely the same problem as all philosophy. 'The problem of the critique of judgement ... is part of the general problem of transcendental philosophy: How are synthetic a priori judgements possible?' (J 145).

Kant offers a 'transcendental deduction' in answer. It is only fifteen lines long, and wholly inadequate. He lamely says: 'what makes this deduction so easy is that it is spared the necessity of having to justify the objective [application] of a concept' (J 147). In fact, however, he argues independently for an a priori component in the judgement of taste, and for the legitimacy of its 'universal' postulate.

Objectivity and contemplation

Kant's concern is, as always, with objectivity. Aesthetic judgements claim validity. In what way can this claim be upheld? While the objectivity of theoretical judgements required a proof that the world is as the understanding represents it to be, no such proof was necessary for practical reason. It was enough to show that reason constrained each agent towards a set of basic principles. In aesthetic judgement the requirement is weaker still. We are not asked to establish principles that will compel the agreement of every rational being. It is sufficient to show how the thought of universal validity is possible. In aesthetic judgement we are only 'suitors for agreement' (J 82). It is not that there are valid rules of taste, but rather that we must *think* of our pleasure as made valid by its object.

Kant distinguishes sensory from contemplative pleasures. The pleasure in the beautiful, although it is 'immediate' (arising from no conceptual thought), nevertheless involves a reflective contemplation of its object. The pure judgement of taste 'combines delight or aversion immediately with the bare contemplation of the object ...' (J 87). Aesthetic pleasure must therefore be distinguished from the purely sensuous pleasures of food and drink. It can be obtained only through those senses that also permit contemplation (which is to say, through sight and hearing).

This act of contemplation involves attending to the object not as an instance of a universal (or concept) but as the particular thing that it is. The individual object is isolated in aesthetic judgement and considered 'for its own sake'. But contemplation does not rest with this act of isolation. It embarks on a process of abstraction which exactly parallels the process whereby practical reason arrives at the categorical imperative. Aesthetic judgement abstracts from every 'interest' of the observer. He does not regard the object as a means to his ends, but as an end in itself (although not a moral end). The observer's desires, aims and ambitions are held in abeyance in the act of contemplation, and the object regarded 'apart from any interest' (J 50). This act of abstraction is conducted while focusing on the individual object in its 'singularity' (J 55). Hence, unlike the abstraction that generates the categorical imperative, it leads to no universal rule. Nevertheless, it underlies the 'universality' of the subsequent judgement. It is this which enables me to 'play the part of judge in matters of taste' (J 43). Having abstracted from all my interests and desires, I have, in effect, removed from my judgement all reference to the 'empirical conditions' which distinguish me, and referred my experience to reason alone, just as I refer the ends of action when acting morally. 'Since the delight is not based on any inclination of the subject (or on any other deliberate interest) . . . he can find as reason for his delight no personal conditions to which his own subjective self might alone be party' (J 50–1). In which case, it seems, the subject of aesthetic judgement must feel compelled, and also entitled, to legislate his pleasure for all rational beings.

Imagination and freedom

What aspect of rationality is involved in aesthetic contemplation? In the 'subjective deduction' of the first *Critique* (see p. 27 above), Kant had argued for the central role of imagination in the 'synthesis' of concept and intuition. Imagination transforms intuition into datum; we exercise imagination whenever we attribute to our experience a 'content' which represents the world. When I see the man outside my window, the concept 'man' is present in my perception. This work of impregnating experience with concepts is the work of imagination.

Kant thought that imagination could also be 'freed from' concepts (that is, from the rules of the understanding). It is this 'free play' of the imagination that characterises aesthetic judge ment. In the free play of imagination concepts are either wholly indeterminate, or if determinate not applied. An example of the first is the imaginative 'synthesis' involved in seeing a set of marks as a pattern. Here there is no determinate concept. There is nothing to a pattern except an experienced order, and no concept applied in the experience apart from that indeterminate idea. An example of the second is the 'synthesis' involved in seeing a picture as a face. Here the concept 'face' enters the imaginative synthesis, but it is not applied to the object. I do not judge that this, before me, is a face, but only that I have imaginative permission so to see it. The second kind of 'free play' is at the root of our understanding of artistic representation. Kant was more interested in the first kind, and this led him to a formalistic conception of the beautiful in art.

The free play of the imagination enables me to bring concepts to bear on an experience that is, in itself, 'free from concepts'. Hence, even though there are no rules of taste, I can still give grounds for my aesthetic judgement. I can give reasons for my pleasure, while focusing on the 'singularity' which is its cause.

Harmony and common sense

Kant valued art less than nature, and music least among the arts, 'since it plays merely with sensations' (J 195). Nevertheless the example of music provides a good illustration of Kant's theory. When I hear music I hear a certain organisation. Something begins, develops, and maintains a unity among its parts. This unity is not indeed *there* in the notes before me. It is a product of my perception. I hear it only because my imagination, in its 'free play', brings my perception under the indeterminate idea of unity. Only beings with imagination (a faculty of reason) can hear musical unity, since only they can carry out this indeterminate synthesis. So the unity is a perception of mine. But this perception is not arbitrary, since it is compelled by my rational nature. I perceive the organisation in my experience as objective. The experience of unity brings pleasure, and this too belongs to the exercise of reason. I suppose the pleasure, like the melody, to be the property of all who are constituted like me. So I represent my pleasure in the music as due to the workings of a 'common sense' (J 153), which is to say, a disposition that is at once based in experience, and common to all rational beings.

But how is it that the experience of unity is mixed with pleasure? When I hear the formal unity of music, the ground of my experience consists in a kind of compatibility between what I hear and the faculty of imagination through which it is organised. Although the unity has its origin in me, it is attributed to an independent object. In experiencing the unity I also sense a harmony between my rational faculties and the object (the sounds) to which they are applied. This sense of harmony between myself and the world is both the origin of my pleasure and also the ground of its universality.

> ... one who feels pleasure in simple reflection on the form of an object, without having any concept in mind, rightly lays claim to the agreement of everyone, although this judgement is empirical and a singular judgement. For the ground of this pleasure is found in the universal, though subjective, condition of reflective judgements, namely the final harmony of an object ... with the mutual relation of the faculties of cognition (imagination and understanding), which are requisite for every empirical cognition. (J 32)

Form and purposiveness

It seems, then, that our pleasure in beauty has its origin in a capacity, due to the free play of imagination, first to experience the harmonious working of our own rational faculties, and secondly to project that harmony outwards on to the empirical world. We see in objects the formal unity that we discover in ourselves. This is the origin of our pleasure, and the basis of our 'common sense' of beauty. And it is 'only under the presupposition . . . of such a common sense that we are able to lay down a judgement of taste' (J 83).

Kant distinguishes 'free' from 'dependent' beauty, the first being perceived wholly without the aid of conceptual thought, the second requiring prior conceptualisation of the object. When I perceive a representational picture, or a building, I can have no impression of beauty until I have first brought the object under concepts, referring in one case to the content expressed, in the other to the function performed (J 73). The judgement of such 'dependent' beauty is less pure than the judgement of 'free' beauty, and would only become pure for the person who had no conception of the meaning or function of what he saw (J 74). The purest examples of beauty are therefore 'free'. Only in the contemplation of such examples are our faculties able to relax entirely from the burdens of common scientific and practical thought, and enter into that free play which is the ground of aesthetic pleasure. Examples of this free beauty abound in nature, but not in art.

The unity that we perceive in the free beauties of nature comes to us purified of all interests: it is a unity that makes reference to no definite purpose. But it reflects back to us an order that has its origin in ourselves, as purposive beings. Hence it bears the indeterminate marks of purpose. As Kant put it, aesthetic unity displays 'purposiveness without purpose'. Aesthetic experience, which leads us to see each object as an end in itself, also leads us to a sense of the purposiveness of nature.

The perception of 'purposiveness', like the regulative ideas of reason (see p. 54 above), is not a perception of what is, but a perception 'as if'. However, it is an inescapable 'as if': we *must* see the world in this way if we are to find our proper place in it, both as knowing and as acting creatures. Aesthetic judgement, which delivers to us the pure experience of design in nature, frees us both for theoretical insight and for the endeavours of the moral life. It also permits the transition from the theoretical to the practical: finding design in nature, we recognise that our own ends might be enacted there (J 38). Moreover, and again like the ideas of reason, the concept of purposiveness is 'super-sensible': it is the idea of a transcendental design, the purpose of which we cannot know.

Aesthetic experience is the vehicle of many such 'aesthetic ideas'. These are ideas of reason which transcend the limits of possible experience, while trying to represent, in 'sensible' form, the inexpressible character of the world beyond (J 175–6). There is no true beauty without aesthetic ideas; they are presented to us both by art and by nature. The aesthetic idea imprints on our senses an intimation of a transcendental realm. The poet, even if he deals with empirical phenomena, 'tries by means of the imagination . . . to go beyond the limits of experience and to present [these things] to sense with a completeness of which there is no example in nature' (J 176–7). This is how Kant explains the effect of aesthetic condensation. For example, when Milton expresses the vengeful feelings of Satan, his smouldering words transport us. We feel that we are listening not to this or that, as one might say, 'contingent' emotion, but to the very essence of revenge. We seem to transcend the limitations contained in every natural example and to be made aware of something indescribable which they palely reflect. When Wagner expresses through the music of *Tristan* the unassuageable longing of erotic love, it is again as though we had risen above our own circumscribed passions and glimpsed a completion to which they aspire. No concept can allow us to rise so far: yet the aesthetic *experience*, which involves a perpetual striving to pass beyond the limits of our point of view, seems to 'embody' what cannot be thought.

Teleology and the divine

Kant attempts, then, to move from his philosophy of beauty to an account of our relation to the world which will be free of that limitation to our own perspective which he had argued, in the first *Critique*, to be a necessary condition of self-consciousness. In aesthetic experience we view ourselves in relation to a transcen-

dental, or supersensible, reality which lies beyond the reach of
thought. We become aware of our own limitations, of the gran-
deur of the world, and of the inexpressible good order that permits us to know and act on it. Kant has recourse to Burke's
distinction between the beautiful and the sublime. Sometimes,
when we sense the harmony between nature and our faculties,
we are impressed by the purposiveness and intelligibility of
everything that surrounds us. This is the sentiment of beauty. At
other times, overcome by the infinite greatness of the world, we
renounce the attempt to understand and control it. This is the
sentiment of the sublime. In confronting the sublime, the mind
is 'incited to abandon sensibility' (J 92).

Kant's remarks about the sublime are obscure, but they re-
inforce the interpretation of his aesthetics as a kind of 'premoni-
tion' of theology. He defines the sublime as 'that, the mere
capacity of thinking which, evidences a faculty of mind transcending every standard of taste' (J 98). It is the judgement of
the sublime that most engages our moral nature. It thereby
points to yet another justification of the 'universality' of taste,
by showing that, in demanding agreement, we are asking com-
plicity in a moral sentiment (J 116). In judging of the sublime,
we demand a universal recognition of the immanence of a
supersensible realm. A man who can feel neither the solemnity
nor the awesomeness of nature, lacks in our eyes the necessary
sense of his own limitations. He has not taken that 'transcendental' viewpoint on himself from which all true morality
springs.

It is from the presentiment of the sublime that Kant seems to
extract his faith in a Supreme Being. The second part of the
Critique of Judgement is devoted to 'teleology': the understanding of the ends of things. Here Kant expresses, in a manner that
has proved unsatisfactory to many commentators, his ultimate
sympathy for the standpoint of theology. Our sentiments of the
sublime and of the beautiful combine to present an inescapable
picture of nature as created. In beauty we discover the purposiveness of nature; in the sublime we have intimations of its
transcendent origins. In neither case can we translate our senti-

ments into a reasoned argument: all we know is that we know nothing of the transcendental. But that is not all we *feel*. The argument from design is not a theoretical proof, but a moral intimation, made vivid to us by our sentiments towards nature, and realised in our rational acts. It is realised in the sense that the true end of creation is intimated through our moral actions: but it is seen that this intimation is of an ideal, not of an actual, world. So we prove the divine teleology in all our moral actions, without being able to show that it is true of the world in which we act. The final end of nature is known to us, not theoretically, but practically. It lies in reverence for the pure practical reason that 'legislates for itself alone'. When we relate this reverence to our experience of the sublime, we have a sense, however fleeting, of the transcendental (T 113).

Thus it is that aesthetic judgement directs us towards the apprehension of a transcendent world, while practical reason gives content to that apprehension, and affirms that this intimation of a perspectiveless vision of things is indeed an intimation of God. This is what Kant tries to convey both in the doctrine of the aesthetic ideas and in that of the sublime. In each case we are confronted with an 'employment of the imagination in the interests of mind's supersensible province' and a compulsion to 'think nature itself in its totality as a presentation of something supersensible, without our being able to put this presentation forward as objective' (J 119). The supersensible is the transcendental. It cannot be thought through concepts, and the attempt to think it through 'ideas' is fraught with self-contradiction. Yet the ideas of reason – God, freedom, immortality – are resurgent in our consciousness, now under the guise of imperatives of action, now transformed by imagination into sensuous and aesthetic form. We cannot rid ourselves of these ideas. To do so would be to say that our point of view on the world is all that the world consists in, and so to make ourselves into gods. Practical reason and aesthetic experience humble us. They remind us that the world in its totality, conceived from no finite perspective, is not ours to know. This humility of reason is also the true object of esteem. Only this is to be reverenced in the rational being, that he feels and acts as a member of a transcendental realm, while recognising that he can know only the world of nature. Aesthetic experience and practical reason are two aspects of the moral: and it is through morality that we sense both the transcendence and the immanence of God.

7 Transcendental philosophy

Kant was regarded by his immediate successors as having irreversibly changed the course of philosophy. But already in Kant's lifetime the intellectual world was torn by controversy over the meaning of his critical system. Was Kant really a Leibnizian after all, as Eberhard had accused him of being (K 107)? Did he believe that the world of nature is nothing but a 'well-founded phenomenon', reality itself consisting in timeless, spaceless, noumenal substances whose attributes are derived from reason alone? Is the 'thing-in-itself' the underlying substance which sustains appearances? In a series of letters to the ageing Kant, his pupil Jakob Beck rehearsed this interpretation, and sought to demonstrate its untenability. But if the transcendental philosophy is not a version of Leibnizian rationalism, why is it not, then, a repetition of the sceptical empiricism of Hume? Kant's philosophy is very much clearer in its negative than in its positive aspect, and in his day he had been called (by J. G. Hamann) 'the Prussian Hume'. In the long peroration that concludes the 'Antinomy' of the first *Critique*, Kant emphasises this negative aspect, and writes with pride of the method that has enabled him to rise above all pre-existing argument in order to show that certain conclusions are not just undemonstrated, but indemonstrable.

Neither the Leibnizian nor the Humean interpretation is really tenable. It is true that Kant sometimes speaks of concepts as 'rules' for organising our perceptions (e.g. A 126), a conclusion that is reminiscent of Hume. It is also true that he is tempted by the 'transcendental hypothesis' of a realm of 'things as they are' (e.g. A 780, B 808), a conclusion that would align him with Leibniz. But these remarks are aberrations. Kant's true critical philosophy can be assimilated to neither of its antecedents, since it removes the grounds from both.

The first important school of thought to arise out of Kantian philosophy was the 'subjective idealism' of Fichte (1762–1814), Schelling (1775–1854) and Hegel (1770–1831). According to these philosophers, the critical philosophy, in arguing away the 'thing-in-itself', had shown that reality is to be conceived in mental terms. Knowledge of an object is construed as 'positing' (*setzen*), rather than 'receiving'. For Fichte, Kant's great achievement was to have shown that the mind has knowledge only through its own activity; in an important sense, the objects of knowledge are a *product* of that activity. Thus Fichte wrote to a friend: 'I suppose I am more strictly a transcendental idealist than Kant; for he still admits a manifold of appearance, but I assert in plain terms that even this is produced by us, by means of a creative power.' The mind is identified with the 'transcendental self', construed as the one noumenal object with which we are acquainted. But who, once again, are we? In Fichte's philosophy the transcendental self becomes a kind of universal spirit by which the separate empirical selves are constructed, along with the 'world of appearance' in which they expend their energies, the whole depending on an unknowable synthesis which generates nature from the inexhaustible reservoir of the 'thing-in-itself'.

Schopenhauer too (1788–1860) was influenced by this interpretation, believing that Kant had rightly identified the 'transcendental self' with the will (which is therefore the true 'substance' behind appearances). For Schopenhauer scientific concepts like space, time, object and cause apply only in appearance, imposing order on the world of appearance (or the 'veil of Maya' – the term Schopenhauer borrowed from oriental mysticism). Behind this veil the will takes its endless, unknowable and unsatisfiable course. Hegel, by contrast, developed Fichte's idea of the known as 'posited' by the knower. He tried to show that the objective reference justified in the transcendental deduction is but the first stage in an expanding process of self-knowledge. Mind (*Geist*) comes to know itself through the positing of an ever more complex world. Hegel described this process as 'dialectical', meaning not to bury but to praise it. He believed that Kant's first *Critique* had displayed, not the errors

of pure reason, but the dynamic process of conjecture and refutation whereby reason constantly negates its own advances,
achieving from the ruin of partial knowledge an ever more complete, more 'absolute', picture of reality.

Kant would have rejected that return to the Leibnizian vision. 'The light dove,' he wrote, 'cleaving the air in her free
flight, and feeling its resistance, might imagine that flight
would be still easier in empty space' (A 5, B 8). Thus he dismissed as insubstantial any pretence to an absolute form of
knowledge, which seeks to soar above the resistant medium of
experience. The notion of a transcendental object is misunder-
stood when considered as referring to a real thing. The idea is
posited only as a 'point of view' (A 681, B 710), in order to
make clear that 'the principles of pure understanding can apply
only to objects of the senses . . . never to things in general without regard to the mode in which we are able to apprehend them'
(A 246, B 303). There is no description of the world that can
free itself from the reference to experience. Although the world
that we know is not our creation, nor merely a synopsis of our
perspective, it cannot be known except from the point of view
which is ours. All attempts to break through the limits imposed
by experience end in self-contradiction, and although we may
have intimations of a 'transcendental' knowledge, that knowledge can never be ours. These intimations are confined to moral life and aesthetic experience, and while they tell us, in a
sense, what we really are, they can be translated into words
only to speak unintelligibly. Philosophy, which describes the
limits of knowledge, is always tempted to transcend them. But
Kant's final advice to it is that given in the last sentence of
Wittgenstein's *Tractatus Logico-Philosophicus*: That whereof we
cannot speak, we must consign to silence.

Further reading

Writings by Kant

There is no adequate selection in English from Kant's voluminous writings. The student cannot avoid jumping in at the deep end, with the *Critique of Pure Reason*. The standard English edition by Norman Kemp-Smith (1929) contains texts of and page references to both editions. The writings on ethics are available in several editions: my references are to the translation by T. K. Abbott, *Kant's Critique of Practical Reason and other works on the theory of Ethics* (London, 1879), which contains both major works, together with an interesting memoir of Kant. *Foundations of the Metaphysic of Morals* is also available in a useful edition (1959), edited and translated by L. W. Beck. The standard English edition of the *Critique of Judgement* (including both the *Critique of Aesthetic Judgement* and the *Critique of Teleological Judgement*) is translated by J. C. Meredith (Oxford, 1928). Other writings are listed at the beginning of this work.

Writings about Kant

The few biographies of Kant make unexciting reading. The fullest, although not the most accurate, is that of J. H. W. Stuckenberg, *The Life of Immanuel Kant* (London, 1882).

Commentaries are legion. A growing interest in Kant among English-speaking philosophers has led to many recent works of high quality and lucidity. The best of these is P. F. Strawson's *The Bounds of Sense* (London, 1966), which contains a thorough exposition, and partial defence, of the argument of the first *Critique*, in its 'objective' interpretation. The 'subjective' rejoinder from Ralph Walker (*Kant*, in the series 'Arguments of the Philosophers', London, 1979), is clear and scholarly, although rather less persuasive. Those interested in a vigorous empiricist interpretation will enjoy Jonathan Bennett's two commentaries,

Kant's Analytic (Cambridge, 1966) and *Kant's Dialectic* (Cambridge, 1974). The best short introduction in English remains that of A. C. Ewing (London, 1938) entitled *A Short Commentary on Kant's Critique of Pure Reason*. Neither the second nor the third *Critique* has received commentary of the same quality. The best that I know in English is H. J. Paton's *The Categorical Imperative* (London, 1947) on the ethics, and Donald W. Crawford's *Kant's Aesthetic Theory* (Wisconsin, 1974) on the aesthetics.

Index

OXFORD

MORE OXFORD PAPERBACKS

This book is just one of nearly 1000 Oxford Paperbacks currently in print. If you would like details of other Oxford Paperbacks, including titles in the World's Classics, Oxford Reference, Oxford Books, OPUS, Past Masters, Oxford Authors, and Oxford Shakespeare series, please write to:

UK and Europe: Oxford Paperbacks Publicity Manager, Arts and Reference Publicity Department, Oxford University Press, Walton Street, Oxford OX2 6DP.

Customers in UK and Europe will find Oxford Paperbacks available in all good bookshops. But in case of difficulty please send orders to the Cash-with-Order Department, Oxford University Press Distribution Services, Saxon Way West, Corby, Northants NN18 9ES. Tel: 01536 741519; Fax: 01536 746337. Please send a cheque for the total cost of the books, plus £1.75 postage and packing for orders under £20; £2.75 for orders over £20. Customers outside the UK should add 10% of the cost of the books for postage and packing.

USA: Oxford Paperbacks Marketing Manager, Oxford University Press, Inc., 200 Madison Avenue, New York, N.Y. 10016.

Canada: Trade Department, Oxford University Press, 70 Wynford Drive, Don Mills, Ontario M3C 1J9.

Australia: Trade Marketing Manager, Oxford University Press, G.P.O. Box 2784Y, Melbourne 3001, Victoria.

South Africa: Oxford University Press, P.O. Box 1141, Cape Town 8000.

PAST
MASTERS

PAST MASTERS

A wide range of unique, short, clear introductions to the lives and work of the world's most influential thinkers. Written by experts, they cover the history of ideas from Aristotle to Wittgenstein. Readers need no previous knowledge of the subject, so they are ideal for students and general readers alike.

Each book takes as its main focus the thought and work of its subject. There is a short section on the life and a final chapter on the legacy and influence of the thinker. A section of further reading helps in further research.

The series continues to grow, and future Past Masters will include **Owen Gingerich** on *Copernicus*, **R G Frey** on *Joseph Butler*, **Bhiku Parekh** on *Gandhi*, **Christopher Taylor** on *Socrates*, **Michael Inwood** on *Heidegger*, and **Peter Ghosh** on *Weber*.